W9-BDL-030

the GASTROKID cookbook

Feeding a Foodie Family in a Fast-Food World

Hugh Garvey & Matthew Yeomans

WILEY

JOHN WILEY & SONS, INC.

This book is printed on acid-free paper. ♾

Published by John Wiley & Sons, Inc., Hoboken, New Jersey
Published simultaneously in Canada

Library of Congress Cataloging-in-Publication Data
Garvey, Hugh.
The gastrokid cookbook : feeding a foodie family in a fast-food world / Hugh Garvey and Matthew Yeomans.
p. cm.
Includes index.
ISBN 978-0-470-28645-6 (cloth)
1. Cookery. 2. Children--Nutrition. I. Yeomans, Matthew. II. Title.
I. Hunt, Mary, 1948- II. Title.
TX714.G3647 2009
641.5--dc22

2008045640

Printed in China
10 9 8 7 6 5 4 3 2

The inspiration for our blog and this book came from the sometimes chaotic, nearly always satisfying joy we experience cooking for and eating with our families. Without the support of our very tolerant partners, Aimee and Jowa, and sporadically culinarily adventurous children, Violet and Desmond and Dylan and Zelda, there would be no Gastrokid. Thanks also to our great agent, Sharon Bowers, for making this book idea a reality and to our editor, Justin Schwartz, for his expert eye and ear. Thanks also to Bernhard Warner for holding down the fort while Matthew was in writing mode and to Barbara Fairchild, Editor in Chief of *Bon Appétit* magazine, for her support of this project from the earliest stages. One and all, they are Gastrokids at heart.

CONTENTS

I cook
therefore
I am

if you're a parent, you don't have time to read cookbooks, which is why we wrote this one. If you don't have time to read the rest of this introduction, then skip to any of the fast, kid-tested, adult-friendly, organic, sustainable, and downright delicious recipes here. They are easy enough to cook on a weeknight and will transform your family dinner into the most delightful and important meal of the day.

For those of you with eleven minutes or so to spare, read on . . .

the gastrokid manifesto:

Gastrokid: noun. A combination of "gastronomy" (the study of food) and "kid." Coined by Hugh Garvey and Matthew Yeomans, founders of Gastrokid.com, a Web site popular among parents dedicated to feeding their children the best food possible. A Gastrokid is a child of heightened gastronomic awareness, sometimes the progeny of parents who describe themselves as "foodies."

all are welcome at the gastrokid table: picky eaters, omnivores, gourmets, vegetarians, cheeseophiles, pizza lovers, food snobs, Japonistes, fish freaks, burger enthusiasts, salad haters, kids, parents, grandparents, babies . . . even those without kids.

We started the Gastrokid.com blog and network to share the trials, tribulations, and triumphs of cooking for our families. We're both working dads with full-time jobs, stressed-out wives, school-age kids, and a love of great food that we want to cultivate in our families. Through the thousands of readers of Gastrokid.com, we learned that we were far from alone. It is for those readers and for you and your kids that we wrote this book.

Many years ago, in the BP (Before Parenthood) age, we used to enjoy our own gastro-life. We were unencumbered food and travel writers who couldn't wait to try the newest Manhattan restaurants; we traveled the world eating the most melt-in-your-mouth ceviche (and sushi for that matter) in Ecuador and embracing the joys of Paisano-chic in Umbria, Italy. We even made it to the highlands of northern Ethiopia to taste traditional injera. Those days are gone (for the moment), but as dads we feel (and, happily, our wives agree) there's no reason why the entire family can't be part of the food adventure we've always enjoyed.

Every kid is born a Gastrokid. It's up to us to feed that hunger and curiosity. If we have just one rule, it is this: Get in touch with your own "inner Gastrokid" and then express your unbridled love for food with your kids. Share tastes at every opportunity and always try new culinary experiences. It's okay for us to say, "It's good to try something new," and it's okay for them to say they don't like it after they try it.

That's why we try not to balkanize our kids into eating separate meals. Also, it's why we do our best to make sure that our Gastrokids eat the same good food that we choose to eat. As a result, our kids gobble down kimchi pancake, Toulousian saucisson, Spanish cured bresaola, sweet garlic and sag aloo, all because we have made it part of their daily eating adventure.

At Gastrokid we believe there's no such thing as "kids' food." Good food is good food to be shared by all. If there's any model we can think of, it's the well-worn Italian one where kids share the table with the adults, where some vegetables, some pasta, and a little meat add up to a well-balanced yet transcendent culinary experience. Wine and conversation flow freely as the children play contentedly, and the evening unfolds at a leisurely pace.

Yeah, right.

Even if that's just a family meal reverie, its spirit lives on in these recipes. All are quick to prepare (most clock in at thirty minutes or less), they're good for you and your kids (organic or free-range, minimally processed), and, best of all, delicious and sophisticated enough that you will need to cook only one meal a night for the whole family. What you eat, your kids will eat, and vice versa, and everyone will be happy . . . until one of the kids starts complaining!

Parents who love good food want their children to love it, too, and it's simply an added benefit that intrepid Gastrokids also tend to be more curious and excited about exploring the world around themselves. We're experimenting and we're flying by the seats of our pants a lot of the time, but we're not afraid to take our Gastrokids along for the ride. Come join us, and let's save the world together, one family meal at a time.

—Hugh Garvey and Matthew Yeomans,
July 2009

"Every kid is born a **gastrokid**. it's up to us to feed that hunger & curiosity. If we have just one rule, it is this: get in touch with your own 'inner **gastrokid**' & then express your unbridled love for food with your kids."

10 GASTROKID RULES FOR RECLAIMING THE FAMILY DINNER TABLE

1. FIND YOUR INNER GASTROKID. Get in touch with the wonder of food. Become a culinary explorer. Get curious about where food comes from: who grows it, where it's from, what its best season is. Talk to your butcher. Learn the name of the vegetable guy at your farmer's market. Get on the Internet and research the history of a dish or another culture's cuisine. Bring your kid along for the ride. Your enthusiasm will be infectious.

2. NEVER CALL A KID A PICKY EATER. If you do, you're only giving them an excuse to refuse everything you offer them. There's no such thing as a Picky Eater, just kids with discerning taste. All the more reason to cook more, to explore more flavors, and not to revert to the quesadilla, pizza, PB&J, mac and cheese safety cycle.

3. DON'T COOK DOWN TO YOUR KIDS. If you do, you might be keeping them from their new favorite food. We once assumed kids would hate anchovies, only to watch them eat one and become instantly addicted to the little briny, lightly bony fish. Offer them a taste of everything. They might hate it, but you never know. And if they refuse to taste, that's fine, too. Never add conflict to the table. There's always a next time.

4. DON'T TAKE IT PERSONALLY THAT YOUR KIDS DESPISE YOUR COOKING. There is often no rhyme, reason, logic, or pattern to the gustatory rebellions taking place in households across the country. It happens at every age: For a baby, butternut squash can go from favorite food to abstract wall art in a single meal. For a toddler, string cheese can suddenly veer from the sole beloved source of calcium to tantrum-inducing object of revulsion. For a grade-schooler, a well-marbled steak can go from favorite dinner to livestock gross-out. And for a particularly sulky teenager, an exploration of veganism might just be an elaborate excuse to be permanently excused from the table—or it might be a valid political choice. In short, taste changes on a dime and has nothing to do with your food. Don't give up.

5. THERE'S NO SUCH THING AS KIDS' FOOD. Once you admit this, you open up the culinary horizons of your household. Do you want butternut squash risotto with sage and pancetta for dinner? Then make it for everyone. And don't ever simply make a quesadilla for the kids while you consider what the adults will eat. Make that kid-favorite quesadilla good enough to satisfy you (by adding, say, fresh cilantro and a mildly spicy chipotle sour cream) and you've just made a single meal for the entire family. For the kids, just hold the chipotle if they find it too spicy. Likewise, if you're ordering Indian takeout for yourself, get a samosa or some naan for the kids. Maybe skip the super-charged jalfrezi and serve the biryani or tikka instead. Nothing should be off the table.

6. WHEN IN DOUBT, ADD SALT, FAT, & ACID. Sounds more extreme than it is: a tiny pinch of salt turns on the flavors of food, suppressing bitterness and making it taste sweeter. Fat can be good fat: a tiny bit of butter for more sweetness. Good fat like olive oil can add richness and complexity (and antioxidants). Acid is the scary word for brightness: the slightest spritz of lemon juice balances food and gives it another bit of contrast. These three tricks can elevate just about any savory dish to deliciousness. Think about how a piece of lettuce comes alive with a sprinkle of salt, a bit of red wine vinegar, and olive oil. The same principles can enliven pasta sauce, roast chicken, or a flat-tasting soup.

7. CARAMELIZE IT. Browner is better so often when it comes to food. A good sear on a steak. A piece of bread that's been toasted. A roasted red pepper. Brown food is more molecularly complex and thus more flavorful. So toast it. Sear it. Grill it. Roast it.

8. EAT SEASONALLY & LOCALLY. It used to be a given; now it's a challenge with vegetables and fruits being flown in from South America out of season. Find a farmer's market near you and shop there: the vegetables will be grown in their proper season and thus will taste better. A perfect in-season vegetable or fruit is convenience food of the highest order.

9. GET YOUR KIDS COOKING. This isn't always easy, but one little task can both satisfy their urge to help, and invest them in the final dish, which is why we've included kid prep ideas with the recipes where appropriate.

10. LOVE THE LEFTOVERS. We live in a world where we discard huge amounts of food, both leftovers and even produce we've left in the fridge for weeks. (Come on. You know you do it.) Make a weekly habit of taking the week's sad produce and making a quick vegetable stock (in a big pot, add enough water to cover the vegetables; simmer for an hour; strain; freeze in ice cube trays and use in sauces, soups, and so on). If you've cooked more meat than you need for one meal, save it and use it in a stir-fry or a sandwich or chopped up and added as stealth protein to a pasta sauce. Or if you have extra veg, consider a good old-fashioned fry up. Even fish can be used the next day in fish cakes. And a frittata never met an overcooked vegetable it didn't like.

When in
doubt add

A NOTE ON OUR RECIPE STYLE

In our households, long gone are the days of leisurely thumbing through cookbooks looking for inspiration, spending hours at the market, getting out the measuring spoons, and constructing elaborate feasts. Here's the nightly narrative now: get home from work, grab a few ingredients, throw them in a pan, and get dinner on the table. Cookbook? We barely have time to cook, let alone read a book. And seriously: what parent has time to measure? A quarter teaspoon of this and a half teaspoon of that simply means two more spoons to wash. And you don't need that.

The recipes in this book are meant to inspire, first and foremost, and eventually to liberate you from dependence on recipes. The recipes here succeed on flavor combinations and ease of prep. It's rustic, rough and ready, imprecise, satisfying. Quite a bit like modern family life.

The Gastrokid Cookbook is written by two dads on different sides of the Atlantic with different cooking and writing styles, hence sometimes very different recipe styles. While we both adhere to the general principles of Gastrokid, our individual approaches—and real lives—are reflected in the way the recipes are presented. These are real recipes that were born of real family meals that we cooked for our kids in the course of our lives. We didn't take time off to write this book. Sometimes the recipe was developed on a hurried night, hence a minimalism. Other times a dish may have been created on a lazy Saturday, which would allow for more steps, ingredients, and detail. Think of it as further proof that there's way more than one way to cook a chicken—or feed a family. And take it as an invitation to make each and every recipe your very own, altering where you see fit.

For those of you who insist on measuring, we've included some measurements as a rough guide, but by no means as a rule. In the Gastrokid foodie family world, there are no rules. If you like your food richer, use more oil. If you like it brighter, add more lemon juice. Don't like parsley? Leave it out. Love parsley? Use all the parsley you like. Unless otherwise noted, each recipe is meant to serve four people.

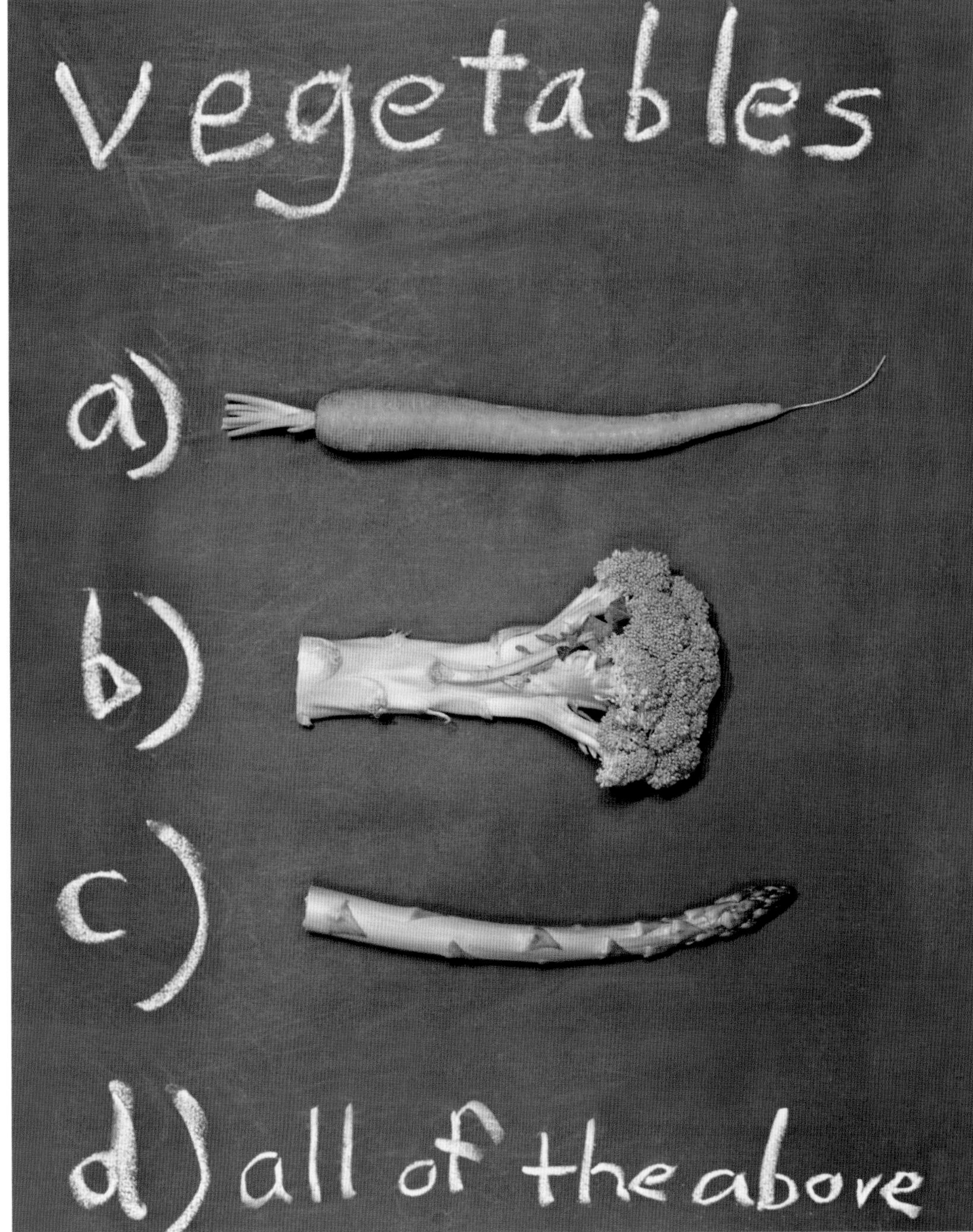
Vegetables
a)
b)
c)
d) all of the above

VEGETABLES

The conventional wisdom goes like this: kids hate vegetables. The reality is this: kids love vegetables —it's just that parents ruin them by buying and cooking them badly, which is why we've made vegetables the first chapter. Vegetables are perhaps the best proof that eating seasonally and locally is a good idea, flavor-wise. When produce is in season it's spectacular; when it's out of season, it's the chore health food that many of us struggled with throughout our childhoods: the pallid industrial robo-tomato complete with Kevlar-like skin and sturdy flesh. The same goes across the board for all produce. Green beans in the winter taste like pencils. Yet eat the right vegetable at the right time, and the texture is perfect. The flavor is nuanced and sweeter than ever. Think of a backyard sugar snap pea in June or corn on the cob at a roadside stand in August. These are the fond memories of childhood, the ones that establish a lifelong love of food at its best. Serve vegetables out of season, and they'll be rejected. Serve them when they're ripe and at their seasonal peak, and they will become beloved.

THE GASTROKID ALL-PURPOSE **GET YOUR KIDS TO EAT THEIR VEGETABLES DRESSING**

There's a reason this is the very first recipe in the book: it's a little lesson in deliciousness and culinary liberation. It's a lesson in the importance of fat, salt, and acid—the three most powerful tools in a cook's repertoire. The three things that will make your kids eat their vegetables. Think about every yummy sauce or dressing on the face of the planet, and it most likely contains fat, salt, and acid—mayonnaise, for one. But if you go drenching all of your vegetables in mayo all the time, your kids will certainly eat them, but they'll also likely end up obese. This dressing is on the opposite end of the spectrum. It gives fresh vegetables just a little lift and awakens their inherent good flavors. We make a big jar of this once a week and keep it in the fridge. Just shake it up to emulsify it (see tip below) before drizzling on salad, raw, cut-up veggies, or steamed vegetables. In spring we love it on asparagus, in summer on tomatoes, and in fall it is a nice contrast to the sweetness of roasted squash. Makes 4 Servings.

- 2 tablespoons or so red wine vinegar
- Salt
- Freshly ground black pepper
- 4 tablespoons or so olive oil
- 1 tablespoon Dijon mustard
- 1 shallot, finely chopped
- Honey

In a bowl, combine the vinegar, a good pinch of salt, and a few grindings of black pepper and whisk with fork until the salt is dissolved. Whisk in the oil, mustard, and shallot and taste. You might find it's just right and won't need the honey. If it could be sweeter or if the tartness still needs to be balanced, add a drizzle of honey.

!

emulsify

Here's a little science lesson for you and/or the kids, as it doesn't involve fire or blades. Emulsify is a fancy word for mixing two liquids that don't want to combine, such as oil and vinegar. While you'll never get them to blend into each other, you can break them down into tiny bubbles that will approach a thorough combination. Whisking very well does this, as does shaking the liquids thoroughly in a jar. A bit of mustard in a dressing helps keep the tiny bubbles in suspension and from breaking apart. If you want a well-blended vinaigrette on your vegetables, mix it just before dressing, since it will break apart over time.

HIGH-HEAT SAUTÉED **BROCCOLI**

Here's the first of three (count 'em, three) broccoli recipes, and our rationale is simple: for some reason unknown to generations of parents, kids will continue to eat broccoli even when they've rejected all other food tainted with the color green. The trick with broccoli (and just about any vegetable) is timing and seasoning: broccoli is at its sweetest just after it has been harvested and declines in flavor as the days pass (another case for buying from a local farmer). A high-heat sear in a judicious amount of olive oil with the right amount of salt is the best treatment for broccoli brought home straight from the market. We like it just like this, but you could dress it up with a spritz of lemon juice and/or copious gratings of real Parmigiano-Reggiano from Italy.
Makes 4 Servings.

- Olive oil
- 2 good-sized heads broccoli, chopped into bite-size pieces
- 2 cloves garlic, chopped
- Pinch of red pepper flakes (a tiny bit will add flavor but not read "spicy" to little palates)
- Salt
- ½ cup water

In a large skillet over medium-high heat, heat the olive oil until it's smoking. Add the broccoli, garlic, red pepper flakes, and salt and cook, stirring occasionally, for several minutes until a bit browned in parts. Add the water and let simmer/steam, stirring occasionally, until the broccoli is tender and the water has cooked away, up to 15 minutes. Taste as it cooks, and you'll know when it's done.

!

why dry?

Here's something the kids can do: have them dry the just-rinsed whole heads of broccoli with a kitchen towel. It teaches the all-important lesson of getting something as dry as possible before browning it in a hot pan. If food is wet, the water will cause the food to steam before it browns.

GRILLED **CORN SALAD**

This is an easy summer enticement for kids to eat their greens. Grill up peak-of-summer sweet corn and sprinkle it on salad and that sweet tart balance becomes delightful for all involved—better than candy corn. Makes 4 Servings.

- **2 ears corn**
- **6 cups or so baby salad greens**
- **1 cup cherry tomatoes, halved**
- **¼ cup feta cheese, crumbled**
- **Fresh lemon juice**
- **Olive oil**
- **Salt**
- **Freshly ground black pepper**

Heat a grill to medium. Shuck the corn and place the cobs on the grate. Cook, turning occasionally, until grill marks appear and the corn gets a bit tender. Once cooled, over a medium bowl, cut the kernels off the corn. In a bowl, combine the corn with the salad greens, tomatoes, cheese, lemon juice, and olive oil and season with salt and pepper to taste.

Salad
gets
Corny

ROASTED **BROCCOLINI**

Super fresh broccolini is skinnier and more tender than standard broccoli and does best with this technique. It's a handy side dish to throw in the oven while you're cooking a pizza: they both roast at the same temperature. Makes 4 Servings.

A couple bunches broccolini
A little olive oil
Salt
Freshly ground black pepper

Preheat the oven to 425°F. On a cookie sheet or roasting pan, mix together the broccolini, olive oil, salt, and pepper. Roast for 15 minutes or so, or until the broccolini is both brown and tender. If you let it go to brownish-black it will become too bitter.

BROCCOLI **PURÉE**

When the handy "little trees" metaphor fails and you've tired of sautéed or roasted broccoli, a purée can be just the thing. A bit of melted butter enriches it and turns it into a more luxurious side dish (say, with short ribs or chicken or pork or just about anything, for that matter). It also works as a broccoli guacamole that goes well with tortilla chips. Don't let the broccoli stalks go to waste. Keep them to add to a salad the next day; peeled and thinly sliced, they add nice crunch and flavor.

Makes 4 Servings.

- **2 cups water**
- **Salt**
- **3 heads broccoli, florets only**
- **4 tablespoons or so butter, melted**
- **Freshly ground black pepper**

In a medium-sized pot, bring the water to a boil and add some salt. Add the broccoli, cover the pot, and cook until tender, about 10 minutes. Drain the broccoli, transfer it to a blender, add the butter, and season with salt and pepper. Blend until puréed; if the purée is too thick, add a bit of water and purée again until the consistency suits you. Some like it lumpy, some like it smooth—it's up to you.

! the power of the purée

Congratulations, you've just mastered one of the simplest ways of thinking about a vegetable in a new way. Puréeing a boiled, steamed, or roasted vegetable into smoothness is the first step toward other dishes, such as soup. Thin out any vegetable purée with vegetable or chicken stock and you've got a near-instant side dish. As for the kids, let them pulse the blender or food processor. Nothing beats pressing a button to make some noise and destroy something.

RADISH, WATERCRESS, **& FETA SALAD**

Feta's creamy saltiness is a great partner to peppery radishes and watercress. Makes 4 Servings.

- About 2 cups thinly sliced radishes
- About 2 cups watercress
- Lemon juice
- Olive oil
- Salt
- Freshly ground black pepper
- ½ cup or so feta, crumbled

In a medium bowl, toss the radishes and watercress with a squeeze of lemon, some olive oil, and salt and pepper. Crumble feta over it all and serve.

! rad radish dish

Once in a while, the clever French are good for a freakishly easy and delicious food idea, such as this one: slather a piece of bread with butter, top that with thinly sliced radishes, and sprinkle it all with sea salt. Uniquely sweet, peppery, and downright delicious.

WATERMELON **& FETA SALAD**

Watermelon is perhaps the most beloved summer fruit among children, and thus the perfect vehicle for other vegetables. Mint and arugula are a particularly well-suited match. Makes 4 Servings.

- **4 cups or so watermelon, cut into cubes**
- **½ red onion, thinly sliced, and rinsed with water to cut the sharpness**
- **A couple handfuls baby arugula**
- **Salt**
- **Freshly ground black pepper**
- **Lemon juice**
- **Olive oil**
- **½ cup feta, crumbled**
- **A few mint leaves, torn**

In a large bowl, combine the watermelon, onion, and arugula. Season with salt and pepper. Squeeze half a lemon over it and drizzle with olive oil. Mix. Crumble feta and mint over it all and serve.

!

definition: garde manger

In a French restaurant the garde manger is, literally, "keeper of the food." The main job of the garde manger is preparing cold foods, including salads. Promote your kids to the title of Garde Manger and let them help with the mint tearing, feta crumbling, mixing, and garnishing.

SUMMER SQUASH, MINT, ARUGULA, **& PECORINO SALAD**

This salad would still be amazing if you couldn't find arugula or mint: the salty pecorino and the thinly sliced squash together are an incredible combination. The trick is slicing the squash super thin (a mandoline helps, but is not necessary; patience and a sharp knife will get you there too). If you want to dress it up and are lucky enough to have squash blossoms at your market, then use the blossoms as a garnish: kids love the idea of eating flowers. Makes 4 Servings.

- 3 cups or so thinly sliced summer squash (slice them into rounds)
- Salt
- Freshly ground black pepper
- Juice of ½ lemon
- Several big handfuls baby arugula
- 5 or so mint leaves, torn up
- Pecorino, shaved into curls with a vegetable peeler

In a large bowl, sprinkle the sliced squash with salt and pepper, squeeze lemon juice over it, then mix. Add arugula and mint and toss gently. Drape pecorino over it all and serve.

!

flower power

Squash blossoms aren't the only flowers you can eat. Nasturtiums and marigolds are delicious too. They add peppery bite and a pretty look to salads. Just make sure you buy ones that were grown organically with the intention of being eaten!

HEIRLOOM TOMATO, BURRATA, **& BASIL SALAD**

This is the king of Caprese salads, that wonderful Italian invention that combines fresh mozzarella and perfect summer produce. Luckily we live in the era of heirloom tomatoes, which means we've got color and flavor on demand in the summer (avoid heirloom tomatoes in any other season; they've likely been shipped from far away and won't have that seasonal sweetness). Add to that burrata, the creamiest of mozzarellas, and you've got a rich salad that needs virtually no adornment, since the juice from heirlooms and the creamy heart of the burrata become a sort of dressing on their own. The salt brings out the flavors and the olive oil gets it all commingling. If you don't have burrata, fresh mozzarella is an excellent substitute. Makes 4 Servings.

- 3 or so heirloom tomatoes, sliced
- 1 ball fresh burrata (or any supermarket variety of mozzarella will do), sliced
- Salt
- Several basil leaves torn into little pieces
- Olive oil

Fan the tomato slices and mozzarella slices on a plate. Sprinkle with salt. Top with torn basil leaves. Drizzle with olive oil. Serve.

glossary: burrata

This specialty cheese takes its name from "burro," which means butter in Italian. That gives you a hint as to the richness of this cheese ball whose outside skin is made from stretched mozzarella and whose center is filled with fresh cream and unspun mozzarella curds.

"The juice from the **heirloom tomatoes** and the creamy heart of the burrata, the creamiest of mozzarellas, become a **sort of salad dressing on their own**."

GRILLED ASPARAGUS, FENNEL, **& PARMESAN SALAD**

This grilled salad is a lovely summer dish: heartier than just the leaves, it pairs well with whatever protein you've got going on the grill. It's particularly lovely with grilled salmon or shrimp. Makes 4 Servings.

- 1 big bunch asparagus, woody base of stems trimmed off
- Olive oil
- Salt
- Freshly ground black pepper
- 2 fennel bulbs, thinly sliced
- Lemon juice
- Parmesan cheese

Preheat the grill to medium. In a large bowl, toss the asparagus with a bit of oil and salt and pepper and grill over medium heat until just slightly charred on the outside and tender on the inside. Then do the same with the fennel (the fennel should retain some of its crunch). Cut the asparagus and fennel into bite-size pieces. In a large bowl, combine the two. Squeeze lemon juice over, mix, then shave Parmesan over it all and serve.

! the fantastic plastic knife

While only older kids should be using sharp knives, it's nice to get some knife skills in early. Use a plastic disposable knife. Once the asparagus is cool, let the kids cut up a stalk or two with a plastic knife. Better yet, you don't even have to buy one: if you pick some up at a fast-food restaurant or picnic and wash them, you've got free kitchen utensils that kids can call their own.

BABY ARUGULA, WALNUT, PEAR, **& STILTON SALAD**

- Handful of walnuts
- 1 bunch arugula, tough stems removed
- Salt
- Olive oil
- Juice of half a lemon
- 1 ripe pear, thinly sliced
- ¼ cup or so Stilton or some other blue cheese, crumbled into satisfying chunks

It's incredible how something traditionally dreaded by kids can become a delight when you play into the season and cook with what's fresh at the market: some greens, some seasonal fruit, some nuts, some cheese, and a simple vinaigrette—plus a well-measured dash of salt. That's the basic formula. Be careful not to overdress it with the lemon juice (just a spritz does wonders) and you might be amazed at how salad becomes a kid favorite in your house. This version is the autumnal take on a basic salad formula, but any combination of salad green, seasonal fruit, nut, and cheese would work (think red leaf lettuce, apple, almond, and Manchego cheese; or baby greens, cranberries, pine nuts, and goat cheese). Makes 4 Servings.

In a small skillet, toast the walnuts briefly over medium heat for 3 minutes or so, taking care not to burn them. On a cutting board, crush the walnuts with a rolling pin or the bottom of a heavy pan. In a large mixing bowl, combine the arugula, salt, olive oil, and lemon juice and toss gently. Top with the pear, crumbled Stilton, and walnuts.

! etymology: salad comes from salt

Salad is the English version of the Italian term "insalata," which means "in salt," as salads traditionally were raw vegetables seasoned simply with salt. We've since come up with more exciting ways of dressing them up, which sort of explains the term "salad dressing."

"If a restaurant like Babbo is giving this away to each and every diner, that's the first sign that this is an **incredibly** cheap dish to make. The **kids love this**. The parents love this. The wallet loves this."

ROASTED **CHICKPEA BRUSCHETTA**

- 2 15-ounce cans chickpeas (aka garbanzo beans), drained and rinsed
- Olive oil
- Salt
- Freshly ground black pepper
- A handful or two chopped parsley
- ½ cup finely chopped olives (I used a mix of some good green ones filled out with super cheap, jarred, martini-style green olives and kalamatas)
- Garlic
- 2 tablespoons balsamic vinegar
- 1 baguette loaf, sliced and toasted

When it comes to coaxing your kids into eating legumes, you could do worse than taking inspiration from a chef who named his flagship restaurant the Italian equivalent of "Daddy." (The restaurant would be Babbo. The chef would be Mario Batali.) This is a rip-off (or what I prefer to call a "riff off," as I didn't have the recipe and tweaked it a bit) of Babbo's freebie amuse bouche (and if Babbo is giving it away to each and every diner, that's the first sign that this is an incredibly cheap dish to make). The kids love this. The adults love this. The wallet loves this. Makes 4 Servings.

Preheat the oven to 450°F. On a cookie or baking sheet, spread out the chickpeas and drizzle with a bit of olive oil. Season with salt and pepper and mix it all up. Roast for 20 minutes or so, or until golden brown.

In a large bowl, mix the chickpeas with the chopped parsley, olives, garlic, and balsamic vinegar. Serve on toasted slices of baguette. The spherical little beans tend to roll off the bread if you're eating too hastily, but chasing down stray chickpeas makes it all the more fun.

! canned food can be good food

As long as it's organic and doesn't contain any additives, having a few cans of good food around can be quite convenient and liberating. Here are three canned foods we always have around:

- Sardines, which we use like tuna (and they're lower in mercury and far more sustainable than tuna)
- Chickpeas, which we roast or add to salads
- Tomatoes, which we use in pasta, soups, and stews

ZUCCHINI **HUMMUS**

Here's an easy way of getting more vegetables into snack time. Serve with the usual pita, grilled tortillas, or crudité for dipping.
Makes 4 Servings.

- 1 15-ounce can chickpeas, drained and rinsed
- 1 green zucchini, chopped
- 1 garlic clove, chopped
- ¼ cup chopped parsley
- ¼ cup chopped basil
- Salt
- Freshly ground black pepper
- ¼ cup olive oil
- Squeeze of fresh lemon juice

Combine all the ingredients in a food processor and pulse until desired consistency is reached.

"Vegetables are perhaps the best proof that **eating seasonally and locally** is a good idea. Eat the right vegetable at the right time and the flavor is nuanced as ever. Think of a **sugar snap pea in June** or corn in August. These are the memories that establish a **lifelong love of food** at its best."

Zucchini
hummus

SAUTÉED **MUSHROOMS**

This is a great side dish or base for other dishes. We've had great success mixing this with a little cream to sauce pasta and using as a topping on a pizza, or on toasted bread for bruschetta. Makes 4 Servings.

- Olive oil
- 2 cups thinly sliced mushrooms (could be a mix of mushrooms like shiitake and portabello, though button mushrooms would be fine and are a lot less expensive)
- Salt
- Freshly ground black pepper
- 2 shallots, thinly sliced
- 2 cloves garlic, chopped

Heat some olive oil in a large skillet over medium-high heat until just smoking. Add half the mushrooms and some salt and pepper. Let sit for a few minutes, without stirring, so the mushrooms begin to brown. Throw in half of the sliced shallots and chopped garlic. Cook, stirring occasionally, until everything is a deep brown all over. Remove the mushroom and shallot mixture from the pan and set aside in a bowl. Repeat the cooking method with the remaining ingredients, then return the first batch of mushrooms to the pan to heat through before serving.

definition: umami

Mushrooms are rich in umami, the Japanese notion of the fifth flavor ("savoriness" is the rough translation; the other four are the standard bitter, sour, salty, and sweet). Chemically it's glutamate, the G in MSG. Work natural umami into the dishes you make for kids, and there's no need to load up with fat and sugar. Tomatoes, anchovies, peanuts, and—naturally—parmesan cheese are umami-packed, kid-beloved foods.

ROASTED ACORN SQUASH **WITH THYME & PARMESAN**

- Olive oil
- 1 acorn squash
- Salt
- Freshly ground black pepper
- Fresh thyme
- Parmesan cheese

Pretty and autumnal and freakishly easy, this makes an ideal side to hearty fish, roasted chicken, or pork. Makes 4 Servings.

Preheat the oven to 375°F. Spread some olive oil on a baking sheet. Cut the acorn squash in half lengthwise, and then into 1½-inch-thick crescents. Arrange on the baking sheet. Season with the salt, pepper, and thyme. Roast for 15 minutes or until tender. Shave Parmesan over it and serve.

thyme travel

If we could have only two fresh herbs in my pantry, they'd be parsley and thyme. Thyme can be used to season just about any protein or vegetable, bringing sweetness and earthiness in just the right amount to every dish. Add the leaves to vinaigrettes; to hot butter to baste fish, beef, or chicken; or to soups and sauces to deepen their flavor.

SAUTÉED **BLACK KALE**

It's the kid-friendly kale: cavolo nero, Tuscan kale, black kale, dinosaur kale—whatever you want to call it. It is tender, it cooks faster than other hearty leafy greens like chard and collards, and it's not too bitter. This is a brilliant side dish, a great pizza topping, or even nice tossed with penne and goat cheese. Makes 4 Servings.

- A couple bunches cavolo nero (see headnote)
- Olive oil
- 2 cloves garlic, chopped
- ¼ teaspoon red pepper flakes (optional for the heat phobic)
- Salt
- Freshly ground black pepper
- Lemon

Wash and drain the cavolo nero. Very roughly chop it into 2-inch pieces along the stem (trim and discard the roughest bit at the end if it's stringy). In a large saucepan, bring lightly salted water to boil. Add the cavolo nero and blanche until tender, about 5 minutes. Drain in a colander.

Heat a large skillet over medium heat, add a little olive oil and then the garlic, red pepper flakes, salt, and pepper. Add the drained cavolo nero and cook for about 5 minutes, stirring occasionally. Spritz with a bit of lemon before serving.

king kale

Here are some darned good uses for this sautéed kale:

- Topping a pizza, along with prosciutto
- Chopping and tossing with toasted pine nuts and goat cheese with pasta
- Chopping finely and mixing into a rich beef-stock risotto
- Serving as a side dish to beef, chicken, or (even better) sautéed duck breast!
- Serving on crostini with Parmesan cheese
- Mixing with ricotta and stuffing ravioli (right, as if you have the time. Maybe on Sunday? That's my favored pasta-making day with the kids. Well, maybe once a year or so.)

CAULIFLOWER **PURÉE**

- 1 head cauliflower
- Butter
- Salt
- Freshly ground black pepper

A most magical side dish, with all the creamy unctuousness of mashed potatoes, more fiber, and less starch. And it's actually quite luxurious: it's grand with pork, chicken, or fish. Makes 4 Servings.

In a large pot of simmering water with a steamer basket, steam a big head of cauliflower until tender. Blitz in a food processor. Add a few tablespoons butter plus salt and pepper to taste. Blitz again, until smooth. If it's too tight, add a bit of water and blitz again.

!

cauliflower power

Buy an extra head of the stuff and try this one out: cut it from the top to the stem into thick slabs and cook in butter like a thick vegetarian steak. Season with salt and pepper.

HIGH-HEAT **ROASTED VEGETABLES**

This is one of those master recipes that will serve you throughout your life, with kids at the table or not. If you take just about any vegetable with an autumnal vibe (butternut squash, potato, cauliflower, Brussels sprouts, green beans), toss them with some oil, salt and pepper, and herbs, and then roast the heck out of them, they will become gorgeously, toastily, unctuously roasty. In summer or spring, you could do this with any firm vegetable such as carrots, fennel, or beets. A bit of Yukon gold or fingerling potato can add a starchy richness. Cook just one vegetable or play with combinations. Makes 4 Servings.

- 6 cups or so of your chosen vegetables, chopped or separated into ¾-inch pieces (butternut squash, cauliflower, halved Brussels sprouts, whole green beans, broccoli florets, or the like)
- Olive oil
- A few peeled garlic cloves
- A few sprigs fresh thyme
- Salt
- Freshly ground black pepper

Heat the oven to 425°F. On a large cookie sheet or roasting pan, toss the vegetables in just enough oil to lightly coat. Add the garlic, thyme, salt, and pepper and toss again. Spread out in one layer, not crowding it too much (you don't want it steaming; you want it sizzling and roasting). If you've got too many vegetables for one pan, put them on two pans, or roast in two batches.

Put it in the oven and roast until the vegetables are tender, a bit browned. Taste about 15 minutes into cooking. If the veg is too tough, too dry, or too bland, add a bit more oil and salt and let it cook longer. After that, taste every 5 minutes. You'll know they're done when they're tender, rich, and intensified in flavor.

definition: the maillard reaction

Named after the scientist Louis-Camille Maillard, this chemical reaction is what's responsible for so much of the deliciousness in this dish (and any other dish that gets brown under heat; brown is the color of caramelization and flavor). Under high heat, sugars and amino acids break down and create new chemical compounds that are incredibly complex and incredibly delicious, which is why a roast carrot or onion becomes so much sweeter when it's been roasted.

FIERCE **POTATOES**

- 4 cups diced Yukon gold or fingerling potatoes (don't bother peeling them)
- A few tablespoons olive oil
- A couple tablespoons chopped fresh rosemary
- 1 teaspoon or so pimentón de la vera (Spanish smoked paprika)
- A couple pinches red pepper flakes
- Salt
- Freshly ground black pepper
- ½ cup mayonnaise
- 1 garlic clove, chopped finely

The Spanish have a way with pimentón de la vera, that magical smoked paprika that makes everything taste like bacon (that's a good thing). Here's a variation on Spanish patatas bravas (which translates as "fierce potatoes"). Patatas bravas are traditionally fried potatoes served with a spicy aioli. This version reverses it, spicing the potatoes themselves, which are then served with just plain old American mayo (Hellman's or Best Foods only—need we say that?). Go easy with the red pepper flakes at first, but you might be surprised by how much your kids like a little heat in their food. Makes 4 Servings.

Preheat the oven to 425°F. On a cookie sheet or roasting pan, mix together the potatoes, olive oil, rosemary, paprika, red pepper flakes, and some salt and pepper and then spread out in one layer. Roast until the potatoes are browned and crisped in places and tender on the inside.

In a small bowl combine the mayo and garlic. Serve the potatoes hot with some of the mayo mixture on the side for dipping.

! secret ingredient: pimentón de la vera

This is probably the single most used spice in our houses after black pepper. It's ten times as delicious as regular paprika because it's been smoked. It can add a wonderful background flavor to sauces, grilled meat, mayo, fish, and just about any other savory food you want to make incredibly savory. Make sure to buy the dolce (or sweet) version, as the picante (or hot) can be a bit much for kids. The smokiness is what makes this stuff so amazing. If you and yours love heat, too, you can always add a dash of cayenne.

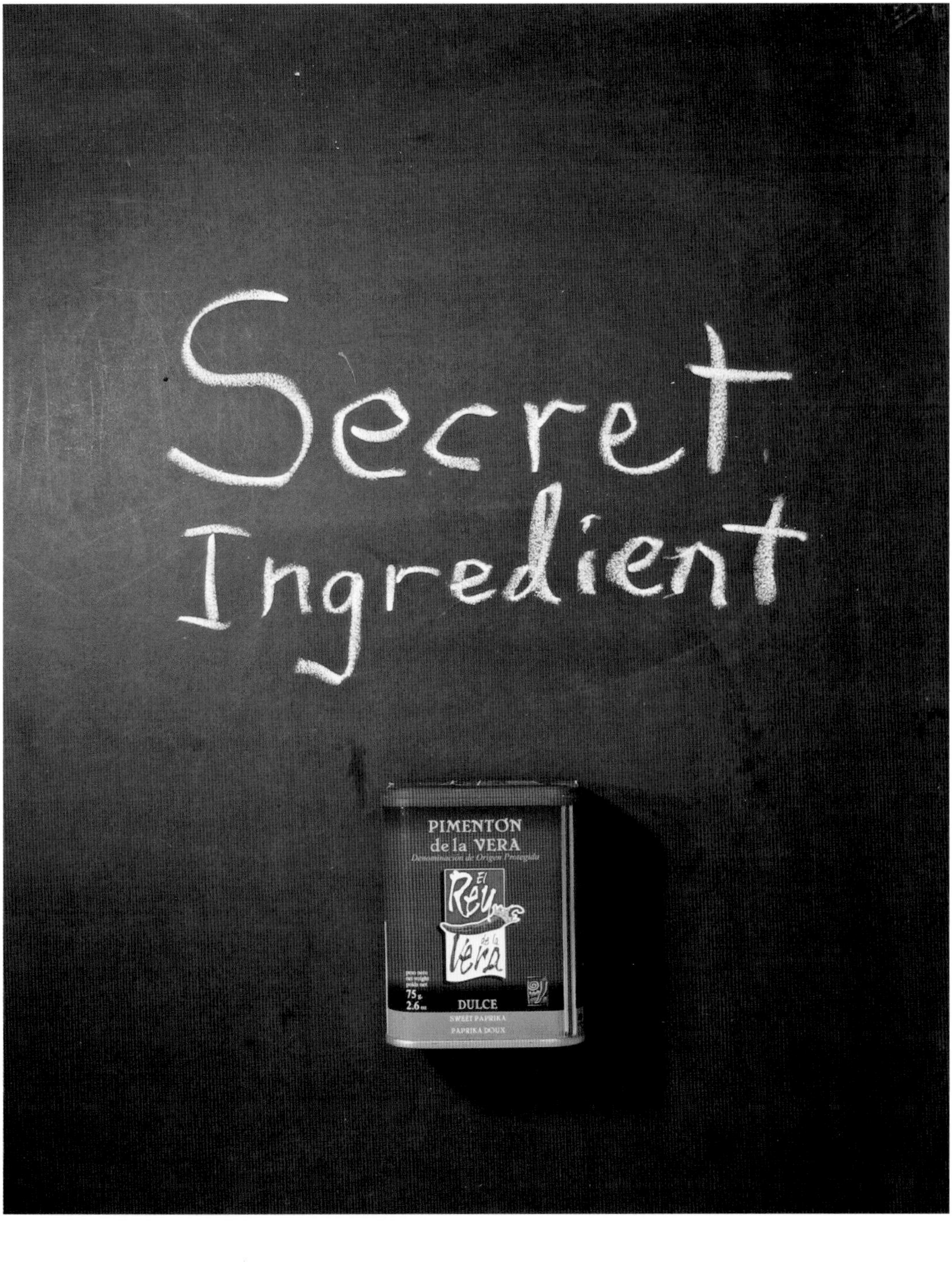
Secret
Ingredient
PIMENTON
de la VERA
Denominación de Origen Protegida
El Rey de la Vera
75 g.
2.6 oz
DULCE
SWEET PAPRIKA
PAPRIKA DOUX

NEARLY INSTANTANEOUS, ITALIANISH **WHITE BEANS WITH GARLIC AND ROSEMARY**

A few canned goods approach perfection, among them canned beans, which need virtually no coddling to make them delicious. Serve with rice and it's a meal. **Makes 4 Servings.**

- Olive oil
- 1 garlic clove, chopped
- 1 can white beans, appropriately sized for your family, drained of that unappetizing thick juice
- 1 tablespoon chopped fresh rosemary

Add some olive oil to a medium-size sauce pan over medium heat. Add the garlic and cook, stirring, for a minute. Stir in the beans and heat through. Stir in the rosemary, let infuse for several minutes, and serve.

!

bean there, done that

Every recipe is a formula, and this one couldn't be any easier. It's basically beans **+** herbs. This can be modified to create any number of other ethnic spins:

- Black beans **+** cilantro **=** Mexican beans
- Chickpeas **+** marjoram **=** vaguely Greek beans
- White beans **+** sage **=** a more autumnal version of the nearly instantaneous, Italianish white beans

SAUTÉED BRUSSELS **SPROUT CHIFFONADE**

The reason lots of people hate Brussels sprouts is because they've been served old and overcooked sprouts. Truly fresh sprouts cooked just through are a whole different story. This technique softens and sweetens them just so. The trick lies in the thin slicing of the sprouts and the quick sautée. Makes 4 Servings.

- Olive oil
- 4 cups Brussels sprouts, sliced thin
- A couple cloves garlic, chopped
- Salt
- Freshly ground black pepper
- Water or stock
- Fresh lemon juice

Add some olive oil to a large pan over medium-high heat. Add the Brussels sprouts, garlic, and some salt and pepper and cook until it's a bit caramelized, 7 to 10 minutes. Add a bit of water or stock. Simmer over medium heat until just tender, 3 to 5 minutes longer; the color should remain vibrant. If you cook until the color goes drab, it's gone too far; the sweetness diminishes and that nasty sulfury taste begins. It's okay if they're a bit al dente. You'll be surprised at the sweetness. Add a spritz of lemon juice to balance flavor if you feel like it.

AMAZING MULTIPURPOSE **GRILLED ZUCCHINI**

Deep into summer zucchini season you need a quick and easy way of making the most of this ubiquitous vegetable. As they often do, garlic and balsamic bring a complex sweetness to this dish. The other trick is to moderate the heat on the grill. Too hot and they'll scorch. Just right and they soften and sweeten, yet still get a nice toasty-tasty char. We eat these straight, toss them with pasta, top pizzas with them, and put them on panini. **Makes 4 Servings.**

- 6 or so zucchini sliced lengthwise into $\frac{1}{4}$-inch-thick strips
- 1 tablespoon or so olive oil
- About 2 tablespoons balsamic vinegar
- A couple cloves garlic, chopped
- Salt
- Freshly ground black pepper

Preheat the grill to medium. In a medium bowl, toss all ingredients together until combined. Grill the zucchini for about 8 minutes per side. You want them tender and with nice deep brown grill marks; it's okay if they're a bit charred, but don't let them get too black.

zucchini management

So you've got all this grilled zucchini, and here's what you're going to do with it:

- Stack some on a panini with shaved Parmesan, arugula, and leftover chicken.
- Chop it up and toss with mint and feta in penne or some other short pasta.
- Chop it really fine and mix into a risotto.
- Chop it up and fold it along with goat cheese in an omelet.
- Grill it up with red peppers and red onions the same way and serve chopped up on a grilled sausage sandwich.
- Or, of course, serve it as a simple side dish to accompany any sort of protein.

GRILLED JAPANESE EGGPLANT **WITH HALOUMI & MINT**

This might be our all-time favorite way to cook eggplant. The tender and slender smallish Japanese eggplant is the least bitter of varieties, and the honey only makes it more kid-friendly. Haloumi is that steaklike Greek cheese that won't melt through the grate of a grill. Can't find haloumi? The eggplant and sauce make an excellent side dish on their own.
Makes 4 Servings.

- 6 to 8 Japanese eggplant, halved lengthwise
- Olive oil
- Salt
- Freshly ground black pepper
- 3 tablespoons honey
- 2 tablespoons fresh mint, chopped (this is for the eggplant)
- 1 piece haloumi cheese (approximately 4 inches by 3 inches)
- 2 tablespoons fresh thyme (or rosemary and/or sage)

Heat a grill (or grill pan) to medium. In a large bowl, toss the eggplant with a little olive oil, salt, and pepper. Grill the eggplant, cut side down, for 5 minutes or so. Turn, and grill for another 5 to 10 minutes, until tender and a bit charred. Transfer to a plate, drizzle with honey, and sprinkle with mint.

Cut the haloumi cheese into ¾-inch-thick steaks. Grill for 3 minutes or so on each side, until grill marks appear, but before the whole thing melts into an unholy mess. Transfer to the plate, drizzle the cheese with a little olive oil, and sprinkle with thyme (or rosemary and/or sage).

all hail haloumi

This great Greek cheese is one of the few that you can toss on the grill or sautée in a pan without much fear of it instantly turning into an oozy mess. Grill it and put on salads and sandwiches, or just eat it as you would a piece of steak, chicken, or fish.

"Green beans taste like pencils in winter. Yet in summer
their flavor is sweeter
and more nuanced than ever.
Parmesan takes it over the top."

GREEN BEANS **& CHERRY TOMATOES**

Here's one dish that is hyperminimalist in preparation. Blanch the beans. Halve the tomatoes. Season. You're done. Makes 4 Servings.

- 1 pound green beans
- 1 pound cherry tomatoes, halved
- Salt
- Freshly ground black pepper
- Olive oil
- Lemon juice
- Shaved Parmesan

Fill a medium saucepan with water, add salt, and bring to a boil. Add the green beans and blanch until tender, about 5 minutes (less if you prefer them slightly crunchy). Drain in a colander under cold running water or in an ice bath (this keeps them from getting mushy and fixes the color a nice bright green). Cut the cooked green beans into bite-size lengths.

In a large bowl, combine the beans and tomatoes. Season with salt and pepper and drizzle with olive oil and a bit of lemon juice. Garnish with shaved Parmesan. Toss and serve.

too many tomatoes?

If you've got even more cherry tomatoes, this idea is just as easy: sautée them in olive oil, salt, and pepper until they blister and pop—instant pasta sauce or side dish. A garlic clove in there is yummy too, but not necessary. A handful of herbs can brighten it all up looks-wise and flavor-wise.

CURRY **UP**

Here's a curry we play around with. It's not a strict formula by any means, but always has an onion, some starchy potato-like thing, some seasonal vegetables, and, of course, Indian spices. It's all about a sauté, a spice, a simmer. We serve it with rice, of course. Basmati is best, but don't fret if you don't have it. Makes 4 Servings.

- 1 onion, chopped
- 1 garlic clove, chopped
- Olive oil
- ½ teaspoon garam masala
- ½ teaspoon ground cumin
- ¼ teaspoon ground turmeric
- ¼ teaspoon ground ginger
- 1 sweet potato, peeled and thinly sliced
- 2 large Yukon gold potatoes, peeled and thinly sliced
- Salt
- 1 16-ounce can chopped tomatoes
- 1 cup coconut milk
- 1 bay leaf
- 2 cups extra firm tofu, cubed
- 1 bunch asparagus, cut into inch-long pieces
- Fresh cilantro

In a large saucepan over medium heat, cook the onion and garlic in some olive oil, stirring occasionally, until tender, 3 to 5 minutes. Stir in the spices and cook for several minutes. Add both potatoes, then some salt, and stir. Add the tomatoes, coconut milk, and bay leaf, reduce the heat to a simmer, and cook until the potatoes are tender, 15 to 20 minutes; add a bit of water if necessary. Add the tofu and asparagus and cook until the asparagus is tender and the tofu is heated through. Taste and adjust the seasoning if necessary. Garnish with cilantro.

Curry Up

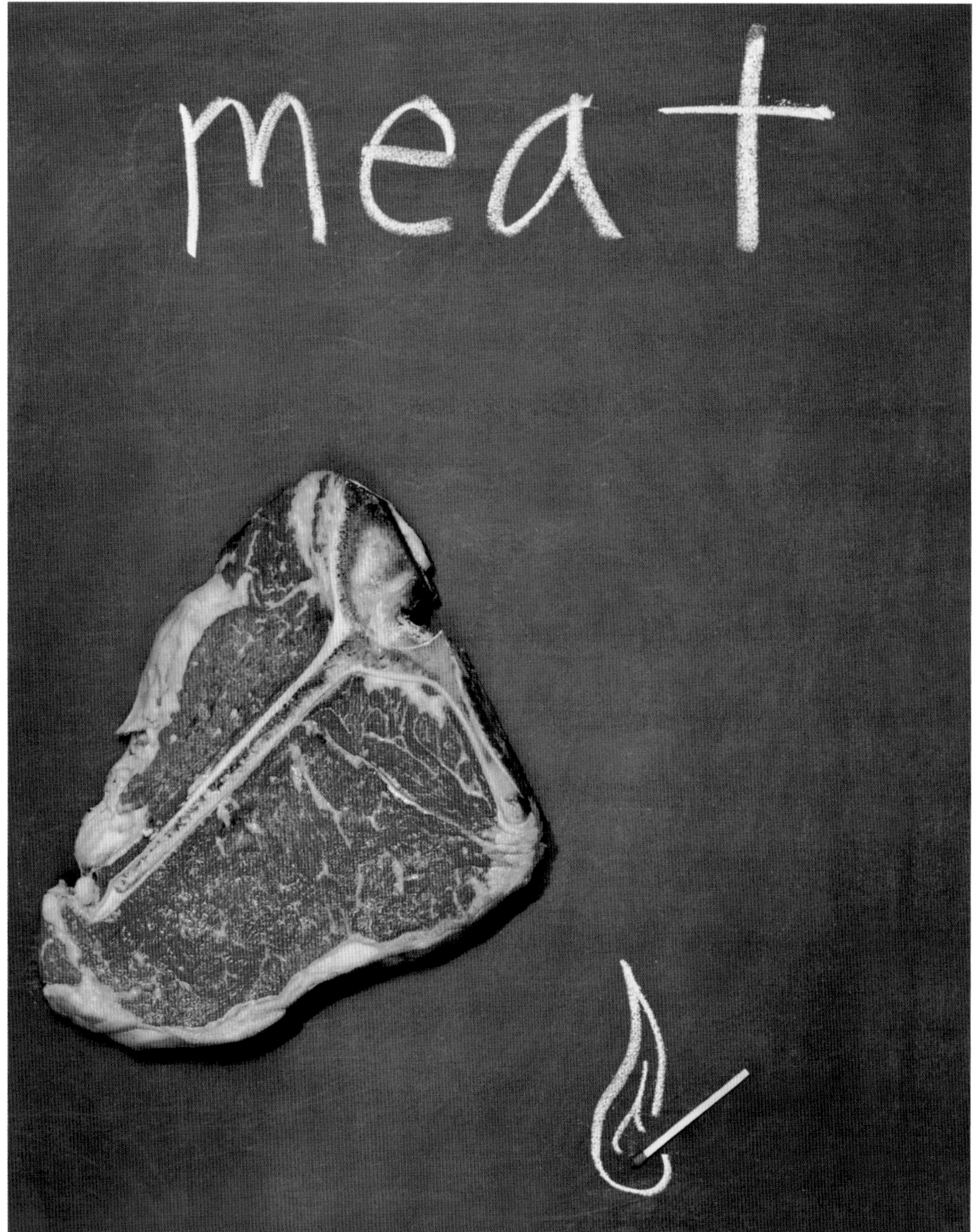
meat

MEAT

How much do our kids love meat? A lot, in that primal way that has them smiling while chewing a medium-rare, perfectly seared piece of porterhouse, bloody juices all but trickling down their chins. They're like little cave babies, thrilled at the success of the hunt. Their enthusiasm is fierce and is not limited to beef, or even lamb. We feed them beef (or lamb, or pork, or, believe it or not, bear—okay, that last one just once) but not in that super-sized, 12-ounces-for-everyone sort of way. We treat meat as a treat—just as it should be and is in most cultures. So steak for our families is a luxury to be savored and recognized as a blessing of sorts. And we'll have just one steak, split four ways, once a week. That might sound meager, but not when you season the meat well, slice it thin, and serve it fanned out on a well-dressed salad of shaved fennel, Parmesan, and arugula, dressed lightly with olive oil and just a touch of fresh lemon juice . . . but we digress. Because we celebrate and value meat, we came up with a series of recipes that put beef, lamb, and pork on a pedestal.

THE GASTROKID **BURGER**

Here's the most important rule when it comes to making a burger: know where your meat came from. If you can't get freshly ground, beef from your butcher, then it isn't worth the juicy indulgence that is a homemade hamburger. While you can certainly play with additions like minced onion and garlic, good beef needs little more than salt and pepper to let it speak for itself. But to take a burger out of the humdrum everyday category and elevate it to the status of celebration food that it deserves, we do have fun with the toppings. Let's not pretend a hamburger is health food. Let's throw some pork fat into the whole affair in the form of nicely crisped bacon. Makes 4 Servings.

- 1 pound ground grass-fed beef (sirloin works, so does just about any other good ground beef; we don't quibble here)
- Salt
- Freshly ground black pepper
- 12 pieces thick-cut bacon
- 2 cups sliced onion (white, yellow, red, whatever you got)
- Balsamic vinegar
- Olive oil
- Buns
- Blue cheese
- Arugula

Mix together, but don't overmix, the beef, salt, and pepper and form into patties. Refrigerate until ready to cook.

Cook the bacon over medium-low heat in a large skillet until done. Set aside (and keep children from eating it all then and there). Discard all but a couple tablespoons of the bacon fat.

In the same pan, cook the onion over medium heat, stirring occasionally, until tender, 3 to 5 minutes. Add a splash of balsamic vinegar and cook for about 1 more minute; this will add color and sweetness to the onions. Season with salt and pepper. Transfer the onions to a plate.

Let the skillet cool a bit and wipe it out with paper towels. Add a tablespoon or so of olive oil and cook the patties over medium heat until browned on both sides. (Or, of course, you can grill the patties.)

Put whatever sauces or condiments you like on the buns, top each with a hot patty, then add blue cheese, the reserved bacon and onions, and arugula. Burger bliss.

!

grass-fed

Grass-fed beef is better for the environment, as it grazes on pasture and doesn't need grains, which require more energy to produce. But it's much leaner than conventional beef, which is why we add bacon and cheese.

FOAMING BUTTER–BASTED **NEW YORK STRIP**

It's amazing how just the slightest tweaks to a recipe can take something already superlative in its simplicity to an even higher plateau. It helps when those tweaks are techniques from two extremely talented chefs: one, a foaming butter with which to baste the beef (thanks, Gordon Ramsay) and two, a last-minute thyme infusion to flavor the butter (hats off, Tom Colicchio). Makes 4 Servings.

- 1 big New York strip steak, or any other steak, such as rib-eye, tri tip, or even hanger
- Salt
- Freshly ground black pepper
- Canola oil
- 4 tablespoons or so butter
- 4 thyme sprigs (yes, leave the sprigs and leaves together; they make a cool rustic garnish)

Season the steak heartily with salt and pepper on both sides. In a medium skillet, heat 2 tablespoons canola oil over medium-high heat (for several minutes at least, so that it gets good and hot, the oil shimmers, and even smokes a bit). Add the steak and cook on one side for about 4 minutes, without moving it, until the steak crisps up and gets nice and brown. Then turn it over to start cooking the other side. Add the butter to the pan; let it melt and foam. Use a spoon to baste the steak with the butter. Add the thyme sprigs. They'll pop and spatter and add flavor to the butter. Baste the steak again. Cook until it's medium-rare (firmish but still springy to the touch, about 4 minutes a side).

Let the steak rest on a cutting board for 10 minutes to allow the juices to settle, then slice into ¼-inch-thick slices and fan on plates. Garnish each plate with a thyme sprig. Goes very nicely with a crisp salad and grilled or toasted rustic bread.

SHEPHERD'S **PIE**

- 6 or so biggish Yukon gold potatoes
- ½ cup milk
- 1 cup grated cheese (cheddar or a cheese blend)
- Salt
- Freshly ground black pepper
- Chopped fresh thyme or rosemary
- 2 tablespoons olive oil
- 1 pound ground beef
- Pinch red pepper flakes
- ½ white onion, finely diced
- 1 piece celery, finely diced
- 1 carrot, finely diced
- 2 cloves garlic, chopped
- 4 ounces pancetta, chopped
- 3 tablespoons butter
- 4 tablespoons flour
- 1 cup red wine
- ¾ cup beef stock (or any stock or water if you don't have it on hand)

The trick to this dish (as with many) is pushing the caramelization on the mirepoix (a fancy name for onion, carrots, and celery) and salting it enough at the start. The frozen peas are completely unnecessary, but nothing says British-type cooking better than pallid peas. It's a homey old-school touch. Oh, and if you want to be truly authentic, use lamb instead of beef (or a mix of the two). Makes 4 Servings.

Boil the potatoes until tender, 15 to 20 minutes, drain, and mash with the milk, cheese, salt, pepper, and fresh herbs.

Meanwhile, preheat the oven to 400°F.

In a large saucepan or skillet, heat the olive oil over high heat. Add the beef, season with salt, pepper, and red pepper flakes, and cook, breaking up the beef with a spoon and stirring occasionally, until browned. Set aside in a bowl. Add the onion, celery, carrot, garlic, and pancetta to the pan. Season with salt and pepper. Cook, stirring occasionally, until the vegetables are caramelized, 8 to 10 minutes. Add the butter and flour and cook, stirring occasionally, until cooked through (that's called a roux; it'll add flavor and help thicken up the liquid you add later). Return the beef to the pan and stir. Add the wine and let the alcohol cook off. Add the beef stock, which should thicken as it comes to a boil (that's the magic of the roux). Pour the mixture into an ovenproof dish, like a casserole or a pie pan. Spoon the mashed potatoes over and bake until heated through and the top begins to brown, about 20 minutes.

!

mirepoix

Are there three more important vegetables than celery, onions, and carrots? The French don't think so, and that's why they refer to this triumvirate of unassuming veg as "the holy trinity." Sautée the combination together (or substitute tomatoes or green/red peppers) and you have the starting platform for recipes from all over the world. Oh, the mirepoix bit? It's apparently named after some French duke.

PORK WITH **CARAMELIZED MILK SAUCE**

This super-succulent pork loin simmered in milk became all the rage after London's River Cafe convinced chic Londoners that a dish needn't be pretty to be pretty darned delicious. Best of all, when the pork is cooked, the milk has reduced into a sweet, slightly lumpy, caramelized sauce that you pour over the meat. It's a bit like having pork con dulce du leche. Now, show me a baby, toddler, or adult who wouldn't go for that. We like to keep the side dishes simple: broccoli and mashed potatoes round out a ridiculously easy but delicious family meal. Makes 4 Servings.

- 1 pork tenderloin (off the bone)
- Salt
- Freshly ground black pepper
- 1 tablespoon butter
- 3 cups milk

Heat a heavy skillet over medium-high heat. Season the pork on all sides with salt and pepper. Melt the butter and then add the whole pork loin and cook until browned all over. (Darn, you could just about stop the recipe right there...with a bit more cooking, of course.) Once browned (taking care not to burn the butter), add a cup of milk, bring to a boil, and then reduce heat to low and simmer. After 15 minutes, add another cup of milk. Cook for 15 more minutes and add another cup of milk. After 45 minutes total cooking time, the pork will be tender and the milk will have reduced to caramelized clumps (trust us, it's far better than it sounds). Remove the pork and collect the milk in a serving bowl. Let the meat stand for 10 minutes, then carve and serve with the milk.

MOD MEDITERRANEAN **BRAISED BEEF BRISKET**

THE RUB

A pinch of:

- Paprika
- Pimentón
- Garlic salt
- Cumin
- Salt
- Freshly ground black pepper
- Red pepper flakes

THE BRISKET

- 5 pounds beef brisket
- Olive oil
- 1 15-ounce can tomatoes
- 1 cup white wine

Thanks to all the Gastrokid.com readers who offered their recipes and tips on the perfect brisket when we queried them for their assistance. This recipe is for them. We took all suggestions, did a bit of mixing and matching, then fine-tuned a braising recipe that is modern, Mediterranean, and ideally suited for the cool-weather months. This is one of those weekend dishes that you get started the day before (the beef needs an overnight rest in the rub) and then starting cooking early the next day (the house will fill with incredible aromas). If you'd like, you can cook it on a Saturday and then reheat on Sunday. It's even better with an extra night's rest! **Makes 4 Servings.**

The night before you cook the brisket, combine all the rub ingredients and, yep, rub the mixture all over the brisket. Cover and refrigerate overnight.

Seven hours before you want eat, preheat the oven to 325°F.

While the oven is heating, add the olive oil to a heavy, ovenproof, sealable pot or Dutch oven over medium heat. Add the rubbed brisket and brown on all sides. Add the canned tomatoes, white wine, and enough water so that the brisket is ⅓ covered with liquid. Place in the oven, covered, and cook for 5½ hours. Remove from the oven and let stand, uncovered, for 45 minutes. The result is melt-in-your-mouth tasty but not spicy beef. Seriously—this recipe rocks.

! beef brisket: slow as you go then serve tomorrow

The key to great-tasting brisket is to cook the meat slowly. Five hours is good but seven would be even better; it all depends on just how organized you are. But perhaps the best thing about brisket is you can do as good New York delis do: cook it a day in advance, let the meat cool, carve it into thin slices, and refrigerate. The next day you warm it with the sauce and serve in an instant. The meat is even softer and more delicious as intentional "leftovers."

ORANGE & GINGER SOY PORK RIBS

- ¾ cup orange juice
- ¼ cup soy sauce
- 1 tablespoon freshly grated ginger
- 3 garlic cloves, minced
- 1 tablespoon brown sugar
- Pinch of red chile flakes
- Salt
- Freshly ground black pepper
- 1 rack pork ribs, cut into individual ribs

Here's one for a rainy day. It's all about good flavors, basting, slow cooking, and the alchemical payoff at the end. Makes 4 Servings.

Preheat the oven to 325°F.

In a large, rectangular roasting pan over medium heat, combine the orange juice, soy sauce, ginger, garlic, brown sugar, chile flakes, salt, and pepper. Bring to a boil and cook until the sugar is dissolved. Place the ribs in the soy-orange sauce, get them fully coated, and transfer everything to the oven. Every 30 minutes, turn the ribs in the sauce to build up a nice lacquer. After 2½ hours in the oven, transfer the ribs to another ovenproof pan, reduce the heat to 200°F, and return the ribs to the oven to keep them warm.

Preheat the broiler.

Pour the soy-orange sauce into a small saucepan and simmer it over medium-high heat for 15 minutes, until the marinade is thick and easy to pour. Baste the ribs with the thickened marinade, then place under the broiler to brown.

EASY SAUERKRAUT **PORK RIBS**

Sweet-and-sour is one of those fantastic flavor combinations. And the acid bite of sauerkraut tempers the super-rich pork ribs. This is a treat best served with mashed potatoes and broccoli. As it's crazy easy, you've got the time to do some mashing. Makes 4 Servings.

- 2 racks baby back pork ribs (organic, 'natch), cut into individual ribs
- 2 16-ounce jars or packets sauerkraut
- 1 cup brown sugar

Preheat the oven to 325°F. Mix the ribs with the sauerkraut and brown sugar in a large, ovenproof baking dish, making sure that the ribs are completely covered (the sauerkraut is key to the recipe because it provides the moisture necessary for really tender ribs). Bake for 2½ to 3 hours. (Our oven is a little unpredictable, so check the meat after 2½ hours—it should be completely tender and almost falling off the bone. This way you get to steal a rib before the rest of the family devours them.)

! the art of efficient eating

Want to know how to do justice to a baby back rib? Give it to baby and watch baby suck it clean of all excess meat and marrow. There was a time—not so long ago—that the idea of discarding any good meat (or fat for that matter) was considered an extravagance. As we begin to reassess our relationship to the land and the real cost of meat, we'd say there is no better time to start encouraging gnawing those bones.

TUSCAN STEAK **FOR TODDLERS**

Of all the cuts of meat in the world, there's perhaps nothing more iconic in that kids' book sort of way than a porterhouse, with its unforgettable T-bone that makes appearances in Richard Scarry stories and Road Runner cartoons. Keep that cartoonish shape and scale in mind when you pick one out at the butcher counter or meat case. You want a big one, because it'll be feeding a family of four. Serve this with the arugula salad, simply dressed with olive oil, lemon juice, salt, and pepper, and some grilled bread, and you've got an authentic and incredibly easy Italian feast. Makes 4 Servings.

- Canola oil (if cooking in a pan)
- 1 huge porterhouse steak (we like to get a really expensive 1½- or 2-inch-thick sucker, though thinner will do)
- Salt
- Freshly ground black pepper
- 1 large bunch arugula
- Lemon juice
- Olive oil

Heat a large skillet or a grill over high heat as hot as it can go. Add enough canola oil to lightly cover the bottom of the pan. It should shimmer, but not be so hot that it's smoking. Season the steak with salt and pepper and then sear it in the skillet on both sides long enough to get it medium-rare. Depending on the thickness of the steak this could vary widely. Cook it for about 5 minutes on one side (make sure you get a good char), flip it, then start testing the temperature about 5 minutes later. My favorite doneness test tool is a cake tester—you know, the thin wire—inserted into the center of the meat. Touch it to your lower lip. If it's cold, it's too rare. If it's hot, it's overcooked. If it's warm and almost hot, it's medium-rare. Remove the steak from the skillet and let it rest for a solid 10 minutes. Don't skip this or you'll lose all the good juices when you cut it up.

While the steak is resting, toss the arugula with some lemon juice and olive oil, then season with salt and pepper. Slice the steak perpendicular to the center bone and serve it on the arugula salad.

MEET **THE MEATBALLS**

- 1 cup cubed bread (crusts cut off)
- ¼ cup milk
- 1 pound ground beef
- 1 overflowing cup chopped fresh herbs (use one or a combination of parsley, sage, rosemary, thyme, oregano)
- 1 cup freshly gratedParmesan or pecorino Romano cheese
- 2 garlic cloves, finely chopped
- 1 large egg, beaten
- Pinch red pepper flakes
- Salt
- Freshly ground black pepper
- 2 tablespoons olive oil
- 1 cup all-purpose flour on a plate
- 1 29-ounce can San Marzano tomatoes (or other canned tomatoes, such as peeled plum)

This is old-school, checkered tablecloth Italian—but better (honest!). You can have these with pasta, on polenta, with bread, on a sandwich, or by themselves. As with many dishes in the family meal repertoire, over time you come up with some principles that secure deliciousness time and time again. So, before we hand out the recipe, a few tips:

- Don't overwork the meat, so when you mix it up with your hands, do so just until it's all combined and holding together. Don't pack it like a championship snowball.
- Season everything: you want some salt in the mix, enough to turn up the volume on everything.
- Use more herbs than you think you should the flavor makes a difference.
- Cut the crust off the bread: you want the light structure of bread, not the added density of the crust.

Makes 4 Servings.

To make the meatballs: In a small bowl, mix the cubed bread with the milk. In a large bowl, combine the bread-milk mixture with the beef, herbs, cheese, garlic, egg, red pepper flakes, salt, and pepper, mixing with your hands until everything is evenly distributed. Using your hands, form into 1½-inch balls.

Heat a big saucepan or skillet with a few tablespoons olive oil over medium heat. Lightly roll the balls in the flour, then carefully place them, one by one, in the hot pan. Brown on all sides, turning with tongs occasionally. To get a good crust, let the meatballs sit for several minutes before attempting to turn them. Do this gently so they don't break apart.

Pour the tomatoes into a big bowl and squish them with your hands (do this carefully because the tomato juice tends to squirt out of the tomatoes as you squish them). Pour the tomatoes over the meatballs and simmer over medium heat until the sauce has reduced a bit and the meatballs have cooked through. Season with salt and pepper.

PICNIC SHOULDER OF PORK, **PUERTO RICAN STYLE**

This dish pays homage to a local Italian butcher shop in Carroll Gardens, Brooklyn, which adapted a pork picnic shoulder to cater to its large Puerto Rican clientele. They never would tell us the marinade recipe, but over the years we've approximated the taste through trial and error. This dish takes a bit of forward thinking—at least 24 hours (though 48 is optimum), since that's how long the pork shoulder is going to marinate in the fridge. Serve with rice and beans. Makes 4 Servings.

- 3 tablespoons olive oil
- 8 garlic cloves, minced
- 2 teaspoons paprika
- 2 teaspoons cayenne pepper
- ½ teaspoon onion salt
- Healthy shake of red pepper flakes
- Large pinch of oregano
- Large pinch of cumin
- Salt
- Freshly ground black pepper
- 1 pork picnic shoulder, about 7 pounds

Mix together the oil, garlic, paprika, cayenne, onion salt, red pepper flakes, oregano, cumin, salt, and pepper in a bowl. Rub the mixture over the pork until it is evenly covered. Place in a plastic roasting bag and refrigerate.

On the day of cooking, preheat the oven to 325°F. Score the fat side of the pork (it's going to provide fantastic crackling) and place in a deep roasting pan, fat side up. Fill the pan ⅓ full with water, transfer to the oven, and cook, covered, for about 3½hours (basting with the pan juices every 30 minutes or so). Uncover the pork and cook for another 30 minutes, uncovered. Use a meat thermometer to check the doneness—160°F—but take care not to touch the bone because that will provide a false reading.

!

tostones

Tostones aren't just a great salty snack/accompaniment, they benefit from little hands helping in the preparation. You'll need six green platanos (plantains), peeled and cut into ¼-inch slices. Heat a skillet with vegetable oil (deep enough to cover the slices), and when very hot, add the platanos with a slotted spoon. Fry until golden brown, but not burnt; you might have to do this in batches. Remove with the slotted spoon and set aside on paper towels to remove excess grease. When they've cooled, have your Gastrokid flatten the platanos with a wooden hammer or similar utensil. Return the platanos to the oil and fry for a few more minutes. Drain again, let cool, and sprinkle with salt and minced raw garlic. Devour!

SAUSAGE WITH **SAGEY WHITE BEANS**

There's a bistrolike minimalism to this dish that is so easy it feels almost criminal to take credit for cooking it. The fresh sage leaf makes it taste fully homemade. Makes 4 Servings.

- About 1 pound sausage (precooked chicken or turkey sausage works well)
- Olive oil
- Garlic, chopped
- 4 cups or so canned white beans, drained
- Fresh sage (or rosemary)
- Fresh lemon juice
- Salt
- Freshly ground black pepper

In a large pan over medium heat, brown the sausage on all sides and cook it through. Once cooked, set it aside on a plate. In the same pan, add a bit of olive oil and the garlic. Cook, stirring, until fragrant. Then add the beans and sage and heat through. Spritz it with a bit of lemon juice to enliven it. Season with salt and pepper if necessary. Serve in bowls with the sausage on top.

"Canned food can be good for you as long as it's organic and doesn't contain any additives. The canned beans **make this bistro dish almost too easy**."

chicken
snack
lunch
dinner
breakfast

CHICKEN

At gastrokid we advocate a reassessment of the way families think about and cook chicken. Not only should it be a given that you buy organic, free-range chickens (to review the benefits: it has been ethically raised, it is hormone free, it has more flavor), but perhaps its time to start treating it as the luxury ingredient it was decades ago, before factory farming. And with the price of a good chicken being what it is these days, it's a lot easier to get with this way of thinking. Though we've been known to resort to a package of the boneless, skinless breast now and again, a whole chicken offers not only richer meat and more bang for your buck (you're not paying for processing), it also is a good way of showing your kids where their food comes from. Old MacDonald is not just a nursery rhyme. It's an instructive story about what farming is all about. Or, at least, what it used to be about. But we can do something about the sad state of animal husbandry in our country. The more you buy organic, free-range chicken, the more you encourage farms to become places you'd be proud to show your children.

HIGH-HEAT **ROAST CHICKEN**

- 1 4-pound whole organic, free-range chicken
- 3 tablespoons butter
- Tons of salt
- A little less pepper
- 4 sprigs each rosemary, sage, and thyme
- ½ lemon

While chicken breast is supposedly a convenience food, it seems half the recipes for it require the reloading of flavor and the reintroduction of fat, which means more ingredients, more steps, and, in the end, more time. I thought: let's get more elemental. Let's get in touch with that most old-fashioned family protein: a roasted whole chicken. Makes 4 Servings.

Preheat the oven to 450°F.

Rinse the chicken and pat it dry. Rub the butter under the skin of the breast, and throw some salt in there. Salt and pepper the whole thing on the outside. Stuff the cavity with the herbs and the cut lemon. Put in a roasting pan and roast for 30 to 40 minutes. If the oven starts smoking and your exhaust fan can't handle it, drop the temp to 375°F. Roast for another 20 minutes or so, or until an instant-read thermometer shows the breast is 165°F and the thigh 180°F. Let rest for 15 minutes before serving.

"We've been known to resort to a package of **boneless, skinless breast** now and again, but a whole chicken **offers richer meat** and more bang for your buck."

JAPONAISE **CHICKEN NUGGETS**

If your kids clamor for the ubiquitous chicken nugget, it's time to redirect them to something a bit healthier and one that you know for sure is organic and free-range. Here's the first of two chicken nugget recipes in the book (the next one isn't so haute, though it's just as delish). It feels almost Nobu-esque to feed your kid these little sautéed treats that use panko breadcrumbs from Japan. Serve with steamed rice and a little soy sauce. Makes 4 Servings.

- Vegetable oil or some other very neutral-tasting oil (try to avoid olive oil here—you don't want the extra flavor)
- 1 boneless, skinless, organic, free-range chickenbreast (that is, both halves of 1 chicken), cut into ½-inch strips
- Flour, spread on a plate
- 2 large eggs, beaten in a bowl
- A couple cups panko breadcrumbs, spread on a plate
- Salt
- Freshly ground black pepper

In a large nonstick skillet, heat the oil over medium heat. Dredge the chicken pieces through the flour, dip in the egg, and then in the breadcrumbs. Sautée the chicken in the skillet (salt it, pepper it, turn it when golden) until cooked through, about 6 minutes a side.

you are nobu

Restaurateur Nobu Matsuhisa is a brilliant chef whom beleaguered parents can learn from. He got thousands of Americans to eat something they didn't want to eat by giving them what they wanted along with it: big flavors. Lime. Salt. Fried food. Salty soy. And he piled that on raw fish. Voilà: Americans became sushi fanatics and the Nobu restaurant empire continues to expand around the world. You too can play this card: give your kids something they like (pizza) along with something they might not be used to (a new fresh herb, a cheese they've never had). Just be honest along the way, and you'll be surprised about the culinary revolution you can start in your own house.

OLD-SCHOOL CORNFLAKE CHICKEN NUGGETS—**BREAKFAST & DINNER IN ONE MEAL**

Here's an old-school favorite, straight from Matthew's wife's grandmother. We're talking chicken fingers breaded not with breadcrumbs—so messy, so much hassle—but with cornflakes. It's basically the American version of the Japanese version, which, when you think of it, is probably the Japanese version of the American version. A chicken-and-egg sort of thing. Or more like, a chicken and chicken sort of thing. **Makes 4 Servings.**

- Vegetable oil
- 1 boneless, skinless chicken breast (again, two halves from 1 chicken), cut into thin strips
- 1 large egg, whisked
- Bowl of cornflakes, crushed
- Salt
- Freshly ground black pepper

Preheat the oven to 350°F. Lightly oil a baking sheet. Dip the strips in the egg, and then the cornflakes, and spread out on the baking sheet. Season with salt and pepper. Bake for 15 to 20 minutes, or until the chicken is cooked through and the cornflakes are toasty brown.

! cornflake chicken nuggets—cereal monogamy

Did you know that new immigrants to the United States and Canada were sometimes given boxes of Cornflakes on arrival (courtesy of Kellogg's)? Perhaps they didn't realize you could just add milk and instead experimented with the flakes in all manner of recipes. Now hundreds of cornflake recipes exist, with the cereal acting as a crunchier alternative to breadcrumbs. Take that as your invitation to experiment yourself: cornflake chicken Parm anyone?

CITRUS-CURED **CHICKEN BREAST**

- 2 oranges
- 1 lemon
- 1 lime
- Large zipper-top plastic bag
- Salt
- Freshly ground black pepper
- Olive oil
- 2 chicken breast halves, each sliced lengthwise into 2 cutlets, giving you 4 pieces total

Boneless skinless chicken breast is quasi-convenient—and entirely flavorless. But this easy marinade will take it where it needs to go. You can serve this all by itself, on a sandwich, chopped up and tossed with tomato sauce and penne pasta, or in a salad. Ideally you should marinate the chicken for atleast several hours, but even an hour-long bath in sweet orange, sour lime, and zippy lemon will elevate this proletarian protein to another level. Hugh's wife, Aimee, deserves the credit for this recipe and makes it a habit of marinating the chicken in the morning, so that it's a near-instant meal come dinner time. Makes 4 Servings.

Squeeze all the citrus into the plastic bag and throw in a big pinch of salt and the same of pepper. Add a couple tablespoons of olive oil and the chicken. Let it marinate for at least 6 hours or overnight.

Preheat the grill (or grill pan) to medium-high. Grill the chicken on both sides until it's done, about 5 minutes a side.

!

salt means sweet?

That's right, salt makes food taste good partially by suppressing bitterness, thus heightening the inherent sweeter qualities of the food, in everything from chicken to vegetables.

Salt is
seasoning

MOROCCAN CHICKEN **WITH APRICOTS, CAPERS, & OLIVES**

This dish benefits from an overnight marinade, so ideally you can prep it Sunday afternoon and eat it Monday night. You've done all the work ahead of time, so it makes a great, easy start to the week. That said, this is a really tasty way of getting your Gastrokids to embrace garlic, olives, prunes, and apricots all in one meal—we even throw some nice, briny caper berries in for good measure. Son Dylan will steal everyone else's olives, so watch out if you invite him around for supper! Serve with couscous. **Makes 4 Servings.**

- 4 boneless chicken breast halves
- 2 garlic cloves, crushed
- 1 teaspoon oregano, crushed
- ½ cup red wine vinegar
- ½ cup olive oil
- ½ cup pitted prunes, quartered
- ½ cup dried apricots, cut in half
- ½ cup green olives, pitted
- ½ cup capers or caper berries
- ½ preserved lemon (chopped)
- 2 bay leaves
- ½ cup brown sugar
- ½ cup white wine

Place the chicken and remaining ingredients except the brown sugar and white wine in a shallow but wide container. Cover and refrigerate . . . and go to bed.

The next day, preheat the oven to 350°F. Sprinkle the chicken mixture with the sugar and add the white wine. Transfer to a large baking dish and bake for 40 minutes or until done.

! lasting lemons (thanks to salt, our kind of preservative)

Preserved lemons are a staple of Moroccan cuisine. We keep a jar ready so we can add them to a dish as needed. To make them, cut 12 lemons in half. Make 2 additional deep cuts into the lemons (as if quartering them) and add 1 tablespoon of salt to each lemon. Stuff all the lemons into a large, sealable glass jar (sterilize it first with boiling water) and add the juice of 3 more lemons so that the 12 original lemons are completely immersed. Close and leave in the refrigerator for a week until they are ready to use. The salt softens the rind and allows the fruit to ferment, taking the sharpness out but still leaving a rich flavor. A small amount normally is enough in most dishes. Chop finely and add to rich meat and fish dishes for contrast and brightness.

PARMESAN **CHICKEN CUTLETS**

The skinless, boneless chicken cutlet is an uninspiring thing, but ubiquitous in its preprepared splendor in supermarkets. While it should be a given that you buy organic, free-range chicken, it is by no means a given that you won't overcook it. And who can blame you? This is perhaps the leanest land animal there is. That said, here's a way of giving the skinless boneless more fat and flavor, and, dare we say, a special occasion deliciousness. Makes 4 Servings.

- 1 whole boneless skinless chicken breast (that is, 2 halves of 1 breast)
- 1 cup grated Parmesan cheese
- 1 cup breadcrumbs
- ¼ cup chopped fresh parsley
- Salt
- 1 tablespoon fresh cracked black pepper (you want a peppery heat)
- 1 large egg
- 2 tablespoons butter
- 2 tablespoons olive oil

Cut each half of the breast into two thin cutlets (or have the butcher do this for you). Combine the Parmesan, breadcrumbs, parsley, salt, and pepper in a bowl. Mix it all up, then spread on a plate. In a separate bowl, beat the egg.

In a large skillet over medium-high heat, melt the butter and olive oil. Once the butter has foamed and subsided and the butter-oil is smoking, start cooking the chicken. One at a time, dip the cutlets in the egg on both sides. Then dip into the Parm-crumb mixture. Carefully place the cutlets in the pan and fry for several minutes on each side, until golden brown and cooked through. Take care not to overcrowd the pan, and cook in batches if you must.

!

brothers in parm

The good folks of both Parma and Sicily lay claim to this dish. Share the love, and the Parm, we say.

FAUX **PASTOR**

The taco is our household's favorite way of using up leftovers: any little bit of last night's protein (be it fish, chicken, pork, beef) can be chopped up, seasoned in a vaguely Mexican manner, and then served with fresh chopped cilantro, red onion, salsa, and a squeeze of lime. The trick is to chop the meat finely, season it well, and then fry it over high heat in copious amounts of olive oil to give it a richness and crispness that allows a little meat to go a long way. Makes 4 Servings.

- 2 tablespoons olive oil
- 2 cups roughly chopped leftover chicken
- Chili powder
- Pimentón de la vera (smoked paprika)
- Cumin
- Salt
- Freshly ground black pepper
- Warm corn tortillas
- Chopped fresh cilantro
- Onion
- Salsa
- Lime wedges

Heat the olive oil in large heavy pan until smoking. Add the chicken and spices. Cook, stirring occasionally, until the chicken crisps up. Serve on warm corn tortillas with chopped fresh cilantro, onion, salsa, and a squeeze of lime.

faux
pastor

CHICKEN AND CILANTRO **WITH PIMENTO POTATOES**

Matthew and family had just come from the Sunday morning market while on holiday in Pollensa, Mallorca, where they'd scored some fantastic sweet red peppers and fragrant cilantro among other great fresh produce. While the rest of the family sipped cafe con leches or licked the first ice cream of the day (it was vacation after all) in the town's main square, Matthew found some fresh chicken breasts to star in my Sunday afternoon siesta-demanding feast. Back at the holiday villa, Matthew made like an old Spanish cook—slicing the potatoes by hand with a sharp knife and raiding the next door's lemon tree to help with the marinade. This dish works just as well when you are not on vacation, but you might need to get your lemon from a store. Serve with the potatoes and a salad. Makes 4 Servings.

- 6 chicken breast halves, skin on
- 6 garlic cloves, thinly sliced
- Juice of 1 lemon
- Olive oil
- 6 large potatoes, peeled and sliced into ¼-inch-thick pieces
- Salt
- 1 large Spanish onion, diced
- 2 red bell peppers, seeded and cut into strips
- Pimentón de la vera (smoked paprika)
- Freshly ground black pepper
- ¼ bottle white wine (we used a tasty, dry, semi-sparkling white)
- Fresh cilantro

In a bowl, toss the chicken with the garlic, lemon juice, and a bit of olive oil. Marinate in the refrigerator for 1 hour.

In a large skillet, heat a decent dose of olive oil (at least 2 tablespoons) over medium heat. When hot, add the potatoes, salt liberally, and turn over to make sure they are covered in oil. Cook over medium-high heat for 5 minutes, turning once or twice. Next, add the onion and peppers to the mix and reduce the heat to medium. Keep turning with a wooden spatula—you want the potatoes to cook through but not burn. Add a healthy dash of pimentón de la vera and black pepper. Keep sautéing the potatoes, onion, and peppers until they are cooked through and lightly caramelized, about 25 minutes. This can be prepared before you cook the chicken and then reheated prior to serving.

Now to the chicken: Heat a large skillet over medium-high heat with a touch of olive oil until it is almost smoking. Take the chicken out of the marinade (reserve the marinade). Add the chicken, skin side down, and cook until the skin is browned, 5 minutes or more. Season with salt and pepper. Add any remaining marinade, along with the white wine. Reduce the heat to medium. Cook until chicken is done and then sprinkle with fresh cilantro.

ACCIDENTAL **AGRODOLCE CHICKEN**

Achieving successful agrodolce (sour and sweet) is considered something of an art in Italian kitchens. It's a universal notion in cooking, whether it is the tangy sweet appeal of BBQ, or the sweet-and-sour dishes of transmogrified Chinese cooking the world over. Matthew's wife created her own little version (perfectly suited for the heretofore coddled palate of my infant daughter) purely by accident when, deep into the swirl of transatlantic jet lag, she spaced on our traditional favorite form of marinating chicken breast pre-pan-fry—namely, a light hour-long bath of olive oil, garlic, and fresh squeezed lemon. All was going well until she reached for the fresh lemon to add to the marinade—we had none (something to do with me being in charge of the shopping while she was away, apparently). Befuddled, she reached for the most obvious condiment she could think of to accompany extra-virgin olive oil—balsamic vinegar. The result after pan-frying for 15 minutes? Deeply tanned, succulent, tart, yet sweet chicken breasts. Accidents will happen in cooking. Hopefully they are all as delicious as this one.
Makes 4 Servings.

- 4 boneless chicken breast halves
- ¼ cup olive oil
- 2 tablespoons balsamic vinegar
- Several smashed garlic cloves
- Salt
- Freshly ground black pepper

Marinate the chicken for 1 hour in the fridge in a mixture of the olive oil, vinegar, garlic, salt, and pepper. Heat a tablespoon of additional olive oil in a large skillet over medium-high heat. Sauté the chicken breasts until browned and cooked through, about 7 minutes a side.

! liquid lunch

Are you tired of dry, boring white-meat chicken? First step: buy it skin on. This will introduce fat and flavor. Then try "liquid," the amazing new ingredient that can add life and moisture to even the blandest breast. That's right, adding some stock or white wine and water when you are pan-frying chicken breasts gently steams delicate meat. Make sure you brown the meat before adding the liquid. Browning not only adds flavor to the meat itself, but also to the pan. Liquid "deglazes" the pan, lifting the flavorful brown bits cooked onto the pan, adds even more flavor to the chicken, and makes an instant sauce. Be sure to drop the heat way down low after deglazing the pan, so that the liquid just gently poaches the meat.

fish
BONITO DEL NORTE
EN ACEITE DE OLIVA
ARROYABE
BONITO DEL NORTE
EN ACEITE DE OLIVA
ARROYABE
BONITO DEL NORTE
EN ACEITE DE OLIVA
ARROYABE

In our homes the kids are fascinated by fish in all their bony, scaly detail. Whether it's touching raw squid (they love the texture), eating whole tiny fried whitebait—eyes, bones, and all—or picking the chunky flesh from the head of a red snapper, our little ones seem unfazed by making that connection between real food and real creatures. It's a long way from our childhood where fish always seemed bland and was sourced from a bag complete with an alien white sauce. We're hoping this new understanding of where their food comes from will make our Gastrokids both appreciative of how great fish tastes and also of what they will need to do in the future to shop and eat sustainably.

COD **ALMIGHTY**

2 tablespoons canola oil
2 cod fillets, skin on
Salt
Freshly ground black pepper

If there's one fish technique a Gastroparent should master, it should be the fish sauté. It's super fast, super convenient, and super healthy (if you pick the right fish). And it's not hard once you've done it correctly and fully consciously (difficult, we know, for your average underslept parent). We serve this with whatever we've got lying around. In this instance we served it with whole wheat pasta dressed with pesto, and baby arugula with lemon juice, olive oil, and a bit of salt and pepper. Makes 4 Servings.

Preheat the oven to 350°F.

In a large ovenproof skillet, heat the canola oil over medium-high heat until shimmering. Move the pan to distribute the oil evenly all over. This could take 5 minutes to get up to the preferable heat. Pat the fish fillets dry with a paper towel, then salt and pepper both sides. Carefully place the fish, skin side down, in the pan and let cook for 5 minutes or so, without moving it at all.

Once the skin is crisped and the fish looks cooked halfway through, move the pan into the oven and cook for another 5 minutes, until the top cooks through and the fish is just able to flake and is no longer translucent inside.

Safety step not to ignore: place a pot holder on the oven door handle so you don't grab the hot handle of the pan once it's been in the oven! And be sure to place the pan handle side in once it's back on top of the stove, leaving the potholder on the handle, which will retain heat!

Cod
almighty

BUFORD-BABBO-INSPIRED BRANZINO **FOR A FAMILY OF FOUR**

In *Heat*, a fine book on cooking in Mario Batali's restaurant Babbo, Bill Buford writes eloquently on the challenges of cooking whole fish on the grill during the dinner rush in a professional restaurant kitchen. The time pressure. The cranky colleagues. The demanding diners. Sounds a lot like a weeknight dinner with the family. This whole-fish dish is inspired by that dinner rush scene. While it may not be quite at the level of the version at Babbo, it's darned near close. And it's not only flavorful, but incredibly primal and fun to dismantle at the table. Here's a vital point not to skip over: make sure you take all the bones out when serving to the kids. Serve with grilled asparagus and grilled bread to keep most of the cooking outside on the grill. **Makes 4 Servings.**

- Olive oil
- 1 white onion, sliced thin as possible into rounds
- 1 fennel bulb, sliced thin as possible, fronds removed and reserved
- 2 garlic cloves
- Salt
- Freshly ground black pepper
- 2 whole branzino, gutted and scaled
- ½ lemon, sliced thin

Heat the grill to medium.

In a skillet over medium heat, add some olive oil. Add the onion, fennel, and garlic cloves and cook, stirring, until softened, about 8 minutes. Season with salt and pepper.

Stuff the branzino with the fennel-onion mixture, a couple of slices of lemon, and some fresh fennel fronds. Brush the fish with olive oil and season with salt and pepper. Grill on each side for 8 minutes or so. The trick to turning the fish over without breaking it apart is to roll it to the other side, over its dorsal (aka top) fin. That keeps the fish from breaking and the stuffing from falling out. The trick to removing the fish from the grill once cooked is either using a spatula as long as the fish (get one at a restaurant supply store or good kitchenware store) or using two spatulas together.

! holy whole fish

Oven-roasting a whole fish is even easier than grilling one. Here's how to riff the above recipe in the oven: preheat the oven to 375°F. Prep the fish the same way. Place one fish (or even two!) on an oiled cookie sheet and roast for 15 minutes, or until cooked through.

SMOKED **FISH PIE**

- 1 pound medium-size potatoes, washed, peeled, and quartered
- 12 ounces smoked haddock (or another smoked white fish)
- 12 ounces salmon fillets
- 1 pint milk, plus extra for mashing
- ½ stick butter, plus extra for mashing
- ¼ cup flour
- 6 ounces mushrooms
- Juice of ½ lemon
- ½ cup frozen peas
- Salt
- Freshly ground black pepper
- 4 ounces Gruyère or mature cheddar cheese, grated

Fish pie is the perfect "welcome to winter" family meal. This is a recipe passed down from Matthew's mum. She calls it Extraordinarily Good Fish Pie, and it lives up to the billing. Makes 4 Servings.

Preheat the oven to 425°F.

Fill a large pot with enough water to cover the potatoes, bring to a boil, and cook the potatoes until fork tender, about 20 minutes.

Meanwhile, in a large skillet, add the fish and milk, bring to a simmer, and cook until the fish is flaky, about 10 minutes. Strain and reserve the milk. Skin and flake the fish; take extra time to remove any bones from the haddock!

Rinse the pan, then add the butter and melt it over medium heat, stir in the flour, and cook for 1 minute before blending in the reserved milk. Add the mushrooms and simmer for 3 minutes. Add the lemon juice, peas, and flaked fish. Taste the mixture and add salt and pepper as necessary (less depending on the age of your diners—that could be younger or older!). Place the fish mixture into a shallow, greased, ovenproof dish.

Drain the potatoes, then mash together with about 2 tablespoons milk, 3 large knobs of butter, ¾ of the cheese, plus salt and pepper. The mash should be very smooth but not runny. Add a layer of mashed potatoes on top of the fish mixture and top with the remaining cheese. Transfer to the oven and cook for 30 minutes, until the topping is golden brown.

To serve, blow on the dish liberally to cool down for smaller mouths, then sit back and admire the apocalyptic devastation as your children devour the fish pie with utensils, hands...whatever they can use to cram it into their mouths fast enough.

"Our favorite way to eat scallops is to cook the big meaty ones in a first pan, served on a bed of cauliflower purée and topped with bacon butter. A simple spinach sautée is a nice side dish."

SEARED **SCALLOPS**

Scallops are the rich (and riche) convenience food of the millennium. They're protein. They're rich. You can sear them up super fast, which means a near-instant in-house date night with a sense of luxury. Our favorite way to eat them is to cook the big meaty ones in a hot pan, served on a bed of cauliflower purée and topped with bacon butter. A simple spinach sauté is a nice side dish. The one downside to the deliciousness of this dish is the priciness of delicious scallops: if your kids love them, it can become an expensive family habit.

Makes 4 Servings.

- 1 stick butter, softened, plus a couple tablespoons for cooking scallops
- 4 pieces bacon, cooked and chopped (a good use of leftovers)
- Leaves from a sprig of fresh thyme
- Dash red wine vinegar
- Salt
- Freshly ground black pepper
- 12 big scallops

First make the bacon butter: mix together the stick of butter with the bacon, thyme leaves, vinegar, and salt and pepper in a bowl and set aside.

Heat a couple of tablespoons of butter in a large skillet over high heat until the foam subsides. Add the scallops and cook until browned, about 2 minutes per side; take care not to overcook them (you want them with a hint of the opaque, not solid white inside). Top with the bacon butter while hot and serve.

SEARED SALMON WITH **SOY-HONEY-LIME SAUCE**

The secret to this recipe is the sweet and salty soy and lime honey sauce which (makes even a simple side dish of steamed bok choy appealing to the little ones.) Serve with fragrant jasmine rice. Makes 4 Servings.

- **½ cup mirin (white rice)**
- **1 tablespoon finely grated peeled fresh ginger**
- **¼ cup rice vinegar**
- **4 tablespoons soy sauce**
- **4 6-ounce pieces salmon fillet**
- **¼ cup honey**
- **1 tablespoon fresh lime juice**

Preheat the broiler.

In a bowl, combine the mirin, ginger, vinegar, and 2 tablespoons of the soy sauce. In a large glass baking dish, add the salmon fillets and then add the marinade mixture, spreading it all over the fish. Marinate for 15 minutes at room temperature.

Meanwhile, in a small saucepan, combine the remaining 2 tablespoons of soy sauce with the honey and lime juice in a small saucepan and bring to a boil; stir frequently until it thickens, about 4 minutes; remember the sauce will keep thickening once you remove it from the heat.

Next, broil the salmon for 6 to 8 minutes, depending on thickness (starting with skin side down and turning halfway through the cooking time). The salmon can also be pan-fried or grilled if you prefer; the same cooking times apply, though you'll want to lightly oil the pan or grill if you are placing the salmon on the direct heat. We like ours a little rare in the center, though we give the kids the well-done ends of the fillet. Drizzle the soy-honey over it all and serve.

mirin, oh mirin

The foundation of many a Japanese marinade and sauce (teriyaki being just one), mirin is a sweet rice wine. When it first became popular some four hundred years ago, mirin was strictly for drinking. Over time it was made thicker and sweeter and migrated from the glass to the pan.

FAST **FISH CAKES**

This recipe was inspired by leftover cooked fish (all the more reason to do a whole grilled/roasted fish; see page 84). If you don't have leftover fish, quickly pan cook any white fish in olive oil. It's British-ish and a lesson in yummy economy. Serve with a huge salad. Makes 4 Servings.

- 2 cups flaked cooked white fish (leftovers are ideal)
- 2 cups toasted rustic white bread, finely chopped
- ¼ cup finely chopped fresh parsley
- ¼ cup finely chopped scallions
- 1 garlic clove, finely chopped
- Salt
- Freshly ground black pepper
- 1 large egg, beaten
- Olive oil, for cooking

Mix all the ingredients except the olive oil in a bowl until well combined. Form into 2-inch patties. Heat a couple tablespoons of olive oil in a skillet over medium-high heat. Cook the fish cakes until golden brown and cooked through, several minutes per side.

! or try this

You can substitute chilled mashed potatoes for the bread. Then roll the cakes in breadcrumbs to form a thin coating. The result is a heartier version of the same dish.

SALMON **SALTIMBOCCA**

One night we were stuck with nothing but some frozen wild Alaskan salmon (not too overfished, they say; minimal mercury to boot). But thawed frozen salmon out of season is always in need of a bit of a boost. We had some prosciutto. We had some sage. We had a thought: saltimbocca, which is usually made with veal cutlets. It worked out perfectly: the full-flavored salmon stood up to the big flavors of the sage and prosciutto (which did a nice job of masking the less than perfectly fresh nature of the thawed fish). And the other wonderful thing about this dish is that it requires virtually no prep, except for wrapping the salmon and sage in a piece of prosciutto—a knifeless task that the kids can help with. Makes 4 Servings.

- 4 fresh sage leaves
- 4 2-inch-wide pieces salmon fillets
- 4 slices prosciutto
- 1 tablespoon canola oil

Put a sage leaf on each piece of salmon, and wrap each piece of salmon with a piece of prosciutto. Heat the oil in a large skillet over medium heat. Sauté the salmon until cooked through, about 5 minutes a side.

gastrokid glossary: saltimbocca

"Saltimbocca" means "jumps into the mouth" (meaning that it's so good, it jumps into your mouth) in Italian. No one ever said the Italians were shy about celebrating their cooking.

"Our **favorite three-minute sardine snack** is a great way of getting some **protein and omega-3s** into your gastrokids diet."

SARDINES & MUSTARD

Here's an almost instant use of sardines, which are not only better for you and the environment (low mercury and not overfished) than tuna, but are also way milder than their reputation, especially the Portuguese variety. Our favorite three-minute sardine snack is a great way of getting some protein and omega-3s into your kids' diet. Serve with toasted country bread. **Makes 4 Servings.**

- 2 cans Portuguese sardines in olive oil
- Dijon mustard
- Chopped fresh parsley

Drain the sardines. Plate and serve with dabs of Dijon mustard on the side. Sprinkle parsley all over.

SHRIMP & **CHORIZO NON-PAELLA**

- 2 medium-hot Spanish chorizo, diced (buy at Latin markets)
- Olive oil
- 1 large Spanish onion
- 4 garlic cloves, minced
- Half a 29-ounce can of plum tomatoes, drained and diced
- ½ teaspoon pimentón de la vera
- 1 14-ounce can chickpeas, drained
- 1 cup water
- 1 pound medium shrimp, peeled
- ½ cup fresh cilantro leaves, chopped

Jonesing for paella (and sadly without rice in the cupboard), Matthew remembered this great dish that he and his wife, Jowa, used to order at a Chino-Latino restaurant in New York called La Nueva Rampa. It was chorizo with chickpeas, and they served it with rice on the side. Here's a recreation of this chorizo y garbanzos dish with some shrimp added for good measure. It has all the essential ingredients of a paella and is cooked much the same, but you can skip the rice since the chickpeas fulfill a similar starchy purpose. Serve with a simple salad.
Makes 4 Servings.

In a large skillet over medium heat, cook the diced chorizo in a tablespoon of olive oil, stirring, for 5 minutes. Reserve the chorizo, then add the onion and garlic to the chorizo-infused oil and cook, stirring, for a minute or two. Add the tomatoes and pimentón and cook, stirring. When the onion is softened, after 3 to 5 minutes, add the chickpeas and water to this sofrito.

Return the chorizo to the mixture and cook for 5 minutes. Add the shrimp and cook until they turn pink. By now, the sauce should have reduced so that it is hugging the shrimp and chorizo. Garnish with the fresh cilantro.

bonus diet: toddler surf and turf

Little palates adore both shrimp and prosciutto. Create a perfect, super quick surf and turf by wrapping strips of addictive prosciutto around jumbo shrimp, grill (or pan sear), and finish with a squeeze of lemon.

LITTLE NECK **CLAMS WITH GUANCIALE**

It's handy to think of clams as a convenience sauce, protein, and garnish in one, since fresh clams are as much about the flavorful liquor inside as the little meat in each shell. All it takes is a quick steam and few ingredients to transform it into a perfect partner for pasta, rice, couscous, polenta, or crusty bread. We particularly love serving it with grilled rustic bread rubbed with garlic and drizzled with a bit of olive oil. Here's our favorite way of cooking them. You'll marvel over how cured pork is the perfect complement to the bivalves: salty turf to the clam's briny surf. **Makes 4 Servings.**

- Olive oil
- ¼ cup sliced guanciale, prosciutto, or pancetta
- 2 garlic cloves, chopped
- 32 or so littleneck clams (6 to 8 per person), washed and scrubbed
- 1 cup white wine
- ¼ cup chopped fresh parsley, plus some more for garnish

In a big pan with a lid, heat some olive oil over medium-high heat. Add the guanciale and garlic and cook, stirring, for a minute or two until the garlic is fragrant. Add the clams, wine, and parsley and put the lid on top. Steam until all the clams open, about 10 minutes or so (discard clams that don't open). Sprinkle the extra parsley over it and serve with one of the aforementioned starches.

gastrokid glossary: guanciale

Guanciale—cured pig cheeks, to be exact—is a delicacy from the Lazio region and considered the king of Italian cured pork (well, if you ask the Laziale). But your kids won't know that, so feel free to use pancetta or prosciutto—whatever you can get your hands on. All cured pork helps elevate the flavors of pasta dishes; as food chemistry guru Harold McGee puts it, "In sum, the flavor of dry-cured ham is astonishingly complex and evocative." We couldn't agree more.

GRILLED **BABY OCTOPUS**

- 3 tablespoons olive oil
- 2 tablespoons fresh lemon juice
- Several garlic cloves, chopped
- Handful of chopped fresh parsley
- Salt
- Freshly ground black pepper
- 4 cups or so baby octopus tentacles (discard the gut-filled heads)

In the coastal Mediterranean, octopus—baby and otherwise—is beloved by children, who are no more grossed out by the creature than they are by, say, chicken. Why? Because their parents were culturally nonchalant about it, much the way we are, with, say, shrimp. Any squeamishness your kids may have about octopus can only be bolstered by your own. To which we say: if you haven't been lucky enough to eat octopus in coastal Greece or Italy, now's the time to adopt a Mediterranean pose at home and make octopus a staple in your house. Serve the octopus with simple boiled potatoes or tossed in pasta.

Makes 4 Servings.

In a large bowl, combine the olive oil, lemon juice, garlic, parsley, salt, and pepper. Add the octopus and marinate for 20 minutes or so. Meanwhile, prepare a grill to high heat. Grill the octopus for several minutes, until cooked through.

OCTOPUS PLUS

The best-ever octopus we ate came from a little restaurant in a Portuguese market town. They grilled the tentacles, then served them with boiled new potatoes drizzled in olive oil . . . mmmm, but we digress. Want to cook super-tasty octopus? (The big kind, not the baby kind.) Boil it slowly in water until the meat is tender (akin to judging when a potato is boiled, say the experts). But unlike a potato, you just might have to boil the thing for over an hour. Then you can pan-fry or grill the deep-sea beast to give it real flavor. Hugh's family's favorite easy octo dinner is to boil one whole octopus in heavily salted water for an hour and 15 minutes, drizzle with olive oil, and sprinkle with pimentón de la vera (smoked paprika) and sea salt. For an accompaniment, cut Yukon gold potatoes into thick disks and cook them in the octopus cooking water. Fresh parsley makes it prettier.

H.M.S.G.K.
"In the coastal Mediterranean, **octopus and squid are beloved** by children. If you and yours haven't embraced these other chickens of the sea, now's the time to adopt a **Mediterranean pose**

I
PASTA
ABCDEFG

PASTA & GRAINS

Pasta really needs no introduction. When it comes to pasta, kids aren't fussy (apart from the ones that are, of course). But while they'll devour it plain with heapings of Parmesan, you, dear parents, might crave a little embellishment. The following recipes are for you as much as the Gastrokids.

BOAR BACON **AMATRICIANA**

- Boar bacon (or pancetta), cut into small strips
- ½ onion, diced
- 1 sweet red pepper, diced
- 3 garlic cloves, diced
- Olive oil
- ½ cup thinly sliced button mushrooms
- 1 15-ounce can tomato sauce (unless you are preparing a fresh sauce from scratch and hence have far more time than the rest of us)
- ¼ cup red wine (reserve another quarter for yourself as chef's friend)
- Hot red pepper flakes
- 1 pound penne pasta
- Handful of arugula/rocket
- Freshly grated Parmesan cheese

In one of those beautiful serendipitous moments when spontaneity meets what's left in the fridge, Matthew came upon the few remaining rashers of the wild boar bacon he scored earlier in the week at the farmer's market. The bacon had been pretty good with eggs, but he realized it could now serve a higher purpose—penne amatriciana chingale.

Fishing around the fridge he also found some sweet red peppers and some of those lonely mushrooms (you know, the ones that get left behind and end up hiding in the farthest recess of the cooler section). Now the cooking could commence. For those seven million of you without easy access to rashers of wild boar bacon, you could joyfully substitute pancetta or plain supermarket bacon and end up with an equally wonderful dish. **Makes 4 Servings.**

In a large nonstick skillet over medium heat, cook the boar bacon in its own fat until it is crispy. Set the bacon aside on paper towels to drain, but keep the fat in the skillet.

Add the onion, red pepper, and garlic with a touch of olive oil if needed and cook, stirring, until all are softened, 3 to 5 minutes. Add the mushrooms and cook, stirring, until they are softened, then add the tomato sauce, red wine, and hot red pepper flakes (depending on your Gastrokid's palate). Simmer the sauce until it has reduced to a decent consistency that will hug the penne, about 20 minutes.

Meanwhile, bring a large pot of salted water to a boil, add the penne, and cook until al dente, following the directions on the box.

Toss the drained pasta with the sauce. Stir in the arugula to add some green color and a nice bite to the dish. Garnish with Parmesan (as if you needed prompting).

! what a boar

Remember Asterix the Great and his best friend, Obelix? That was a favorite comic back when we were young, and whenever there's boar on the menu, it takes us back to the wild boar feasts Asterix and Co. would devour. They knew what they were doing: boar is best.

PANCETTA SQUASH **& KALE RISOTTO**

- 6 cups chicken stock or hot water, kept simmering
- ¼ pound pancetta, chopped
- Olive oil
- 1 bunch fresh kale, stems cut off and discarded and the rest chopped
- 1 butternut squash, peeled and cubed
- Salt
- Freshly ground black pepper
- 1 cup Arborio rice
- ¼ cup white wine
- ¼ cup freshly grated Parmesan cheese

Getting kids to eat butternut squash and kale all in one dish? It's easy when there's pancetta and Parmesan involved. This is a great fall risotto, and the squash really captures the season. Makes 4 Servings.

Risotto is a time-intensive operation made easy by some efficient up-front preparation. So, first heat up 6 cups of chicken stock in a medium saucepan over low heat, so it's hot but not simmering. If you don't have chicken stock, do what we often do: throw a tablespoon of soy sauce into 6 cups of water. It seasons it and gives depth of flavor, but doesn't make it taste soy-saucey.

Then, in a very large skillet, large saucepan, or paella pan, add the pancetta with a little olive oil over medium heat and cook, stirring, for a couple of minutes. Add the kale and cook, stirring occasionally, for another 5 minutes. Remove the pancetta and the kale and set aside in a medium bowl. Add some more olive oil to the bacony base in the pan and, when hot, add the cubed squash. Season with salt and pepper. Cook for another 5 minutes, stirring, and then throw in the rice and stir for a minute, making sure it is coated sufficiently with the olive oil.

Raise the heat to medium-high, add the wine, and let cook until absorbed by the rice, stirring occasionally. Add 2 ladles of the hot stock/water and cook, stirring, until the rice has absorbed nearly all the liquid. Then add 2 more ladles. Repeat. Repeat. Repeat, until the rice is al dente and the squash is soft but still holding together. This could take anywhere from 15 to 30 minutes, depending on all the variables.

Add 1 more ladle of liquid, then reintroduce the pancetta and kale and stir together. Now add the Parmesan cheese, keeping a small amount for little minds to add after (just in case they don't believe you when you say there's cheese in it already). Serve, sit back, and believe your eyes. Kids really do like kale and squash!

50/50 **PASTA**

Olive oil
1 little can anchovies
3 garlic cloves, minced
Big pinch red pepper flakes
6 cups roughly chopped broccoli and cauliflower
Salt
Freshly ground black pepper
1 pound spaghetti
Freshly grated Parmesan cheese

Weary of cooking a main and side, we decided to combine the two in one, in a vegetable-rich pasta that benefits from copious amounts of olive oil, anchovies for stealthy depth of flavor, and nice long caramelization in the pan. The main components are cruciferous vegetables (in this case broccoli and cauliflower. We prefer orange and purple of the latter for fun at the market, but you can use any color you like). This dish tosses the whole Italian notion of minimal sauce out the window. This is a ratio of about 50/50 pasta to vegetables—and this is a good way of getting you and yours to eat theirs and love it while they do. Makes 4 Servings.

Get a large pot of salted water boiling.

Heat more olive oil than you're inclined to in a large skillet over medium heat. Add the anchovies, garlic, and red pepper flakes and cook, stirring with a wooden spoon to break up the anchovies. Stir in the vegetables and let sit over the heat until they start to caramelize a bit, about 8 minutes. Salt and pepper the vegetables, then cook, stirring once in a while until they start to soften, about 8 minutes more. Stir in ½ cup of water to soften them further. Cook until the vegetables are tasty and tender and have broken down to the point that they'll meld nicely with the pasta. Add more water if necessary.

Meanwhile, cook the pasta until al dente, according to the package directions. Add enough of the drained spaghetti to the pan so that you've got a nice balance of the two. Plate it. Parm it.

PORK & **MUSHROOM RAGU**

This is about as rich and savory as meat sauces get. Perfect in autumn or winter. We like to serve this as a topping for flat, wide pappardelle, though it honestly is sticky and rich enough to go well with any hardy shape. Just avoid anything super delicate like a spaghettini or angel hair. Makes 4 Servings.

- Olive oil
- 2 cups button mushrooms, finely chopped
- Salt
- Freshly ground black pepper
- ½ cup red onion, chopped
- 1 garlic clove, chopped
- Red pepper flakes
- ¾ pound ground pork
- Fresh sage, chopped
- Fresh thyme, chopped
- Fresh rosemary, chopped
- 1 16-ounce can plum tomatoes

Add some olive oil to a large saucepan over medium heat. Add the mushrooms and some salt and pepper and cook, stirring, until softened. Remove from the pan and set aside. Add a little more olive oil to the pan and then the onion, garlic, and red pepper flakes. Cook, stirring, until the onion is translucent, 3 to 5 minutes.

Add the ground pork, breaking it up with a spoon. Season with salt and pepper. Add the mushrooms back to the pan, along with the chopped herbs. Break up the tomatoes into small pieces with your hands and add the tomatoes and juices to the pan. Cook over low heat for 2 hours, until everything is melded and lovely. Serve over pasta with grated Parmesan cheese.

gastrokid glossary: pasta terminology

The Italians love giving descriptive names to their pasta. Here's a guide to some of our quirky favorites:

Armoniche—ridged pasta shapes that look like harmonicas

Conchiglie—Italian for "shells"

Farfalle—Italian for "butterflies," sometimes called bow ties

Fettuccine—Italian for "ribbons"

Gemelli—Italian for "twins," pasta shapes made from two strands twisted around each other

Linguine—Italian for "small tongues"

Mezzelune—Italian for "half moons"

Orecchiette—Italian for "little ears"

Penne—Italian for "quills," tubes whose angled ends look like pen nibs

"The gnudi at the Spotted Pig in New York is pillowy, unctuous and seemingly weightless, despite being loaded with sagey brown butter. Refrain from Big Macs, and once in awhile a dish like this is ideal."

GNUDI

We've recently been experimenting with variations on the gnudi from Spotted Pig restaurant in New York City. This version there is made with sheep's milk ricotta, which we have no easy access to. The version at the Spotted Pig is light, pillowy, unctuous, and somehow seemingly weightless, despite being loaded with fat and sauced with about a ¼ cup of sagey brown butter. This stuff is by no means healthy, but if you refrain from feeding your kids Big Macs and the like, once in a while a dish like this is ideal. The kids adore it. But then again, much like all children, they are cheese freaks. **Makes 4 Servings.**

- 15 ounces ricotta, drained
- 1 large egg, beaten
- ¾ cup flour
- Salt
- Freshly ground black pepper
- A few gratings nutmeg
- ½ stick butter
- 12 or so sage leaves
- ¼ cup grated Parmesan or pecorino cheese

In a large bowl mix together the ricotta, egg, flour, salt, pepper, and nutmeg until just combined. Using a tablespoon, scoop up a good measure of the mixture and roll into a sphere, much like making a little ricotta snowball roughly 1½ inches in diameter. Place on a floured surface. Repeat until you have a whole mess of little gnudi, made in as uniform a size and shape as possible. At this point you should refrigerate the gnudi for at least a half hour before proceeding. You can also freeze them for future use.

Bring a pot of salted water to a gentle boil, add the gnudi, and cook until they float to the surface.

While the gnudi are gently boiling, melt the butter in a saucepan until it has foamed, the foam has subsided, and the butter starts to turn a honeyed sort of brown. Add the sage leaves and cook, stirring a bit, until super fragrant and a bit crisp.

Once the gnudi is cooked, divide it among bowls and then top with the browned sage butter, with the crispy sage as a garnish. Top with a serious grating of Parmesan. Serve immediately to deafening applause from children of all ages.

FULLY MAXIMIZED HOMEMADE MAC & CHEESE WITH **PROSCIUTTO, PAN-ROASTED TOMATOES, & CRISPY SAGE**

- 1 pound penne, or little shells, or rigatoni
- 2 tablespoons olive oil
- 8 or so fresh whole sage leaves
- Salt
- Freshly ground black pepper
- ¼ cup prosciutto, roughly chopped
- 1 cup cherry tomatoes
- 3 tablespoons butter
- 2 tablespoons flour
- ½ cup heavy cream
- 5 cups grated cheese such as a 4-cheese blend, or 1¼ cups each Parmesan, Gruyère, Asiago, cheddar, or whatever ratio you like

This exceptional version of mac and cheese takes a bit longer than the boxed stuff, natch, but is worth it. The better cheese you buy, the better it will taste (and a portion of sharp cheddar can offset the extreme richness of the dish). This recipe is proof that homemade reigns supreme. The pan-roasted tomatoes add just a bit of tanginess and melt into the cheese when you cut into them. The sage and prosciutto knock it out of the park. Grating Parmesan over the top at the end is optional, delirious overkill. Makes 6 Servings.

Preheat the oven to 375°F. Butter an approximately 8 x 11 x 2-inch deep, oven-ready baking dish or casserole. In a large pot, cook the pasta until al-dente in boiling salted water, drain, and set aside.

Meanwhile, in a large saucepan over medium-high heat, add the olive oil and fry the whole sage leaves until crisp but still green, about 3 minutes. Remove the sage from the pan and season with salt and pepper. Add the prosciutto and cherry tomatoes to the pan and fry, stirring occasionally, until the prosciutto is crisp and the tomatoes lightly browned but not totally mushy. Using a slotted spoon (or any large spoon for that matter), remove the prosciutto and tomatoes from the pan and set aside. Add the butter to the pan and let it melt, then add the flour and stir, cooking until lightly browned. Stir in the cream.

In a large bowl, combine the grated cheese, cream mixture, and pasta. Gently mix it up until the cheese and cream mixture are well distributed, adding a bit more cream if it seems too dry. Season with pepper and add a bit of salt if necessary. Pour the mixture into the prepared baking dish. Top with the tomatoes, sage, and prosciutto. Bake for 30 minutes or until the whole thing is bubbly and a bit browned in spots. Serve, grating Parmesan over the top of each serving if you'd like.

MAC & **CHEESE MAXIMUS**

There are moments in a foodie parent's life when the best artisanal, slow foodist intentions can't compete with a kid (or a parent, for that matter) crashing from low blood sugar levels. Dinner can sometimes have a way of ambushing you. Luckily, in most foodie parents' cupboards there's usually a box or two of Annie's brand microwavable mac and cheese, which at the very least uses organic pasta. Sure, just because it's organic doesn't mean it's hyper-nutritious (organic or not, mac and cheese is just starch and fat and trace protein), but here are two extremely easy riffs to take it beyond the basic: one leans healthy, one leans haute.

Makes 4 Servings.

INSTANT SPINACH MAC & CHEESE

Stir in finely chopped spinach so that it fully melds with the cheese and coats the noodles with its fibrous, ferrous goodness and cannot be picked out.

INSTANT TRUFFLED MAC & CHEESE

Boost the umami appeal of the mac and cheese with a few drops of white truffle oil, some chopped prosciutto, finely chopped parsley, and a grating of fresh Parmesan cheese. I'm telling you, you'd even eat this yourself (with a glass of Barbera d'Alba perhaps?).

SOMEWHAT **FAST BOLOGNESE**

For years we subscribed to the Marcella Hazan philosophy of cooking Bolognese sauce: cook it slow and low until everything breaks down into an unctuous, meaty, barely tomatoey, orange-with-fat ragu. She suggests something like three or four hours. Indeed, things do meld in a magical way over a time span like that. Meat breaks down into a most lovely, yielding, pasta-coating substance. Things get sweet. The tang of the white wine and the barely there tomato somehow stand out in its subtlety. It's pretty great.

But what parent has four hours to spare? Not us. We'd actually turned this peasant dish into a special-occasion-preparation, once-a-year, Christmas Eve tradition. We'd start cooking it well before the kids went to sleep and then eat it before doing the finishing touches on gift wrapping and toy assembly.

We recently read about a sautéed variation on Bolognese, in which the sauce is basically fried in enough fat to get everything caramelized and melded at the high end of the temperature range. The opposite of slow and low, but with supposedly excellent results. There wasn't a recipe, so we gave it a shot. It worked. You'd never know it didn't take four hours. Makes 4 Servings.

- 5 tablespoons olive oil
- 1 pound ground beef, not too lean
- 1 white onion, finely chopped
- 2 celery stalks, finely chopped
- 1 big carrot, finely chopped
- ¼ cup pancetta or prosciutto, finely chopped (you can use bacon, but that adds a smoky note that can be a bit overpowering, although still darned good)
- Salt
- Freshly ground black pepper
- ¼ cup white wine
- 2 cups canned peeled whole tomatoes, crushed with your hand

Heat 2 tablespoons of the olive oil in a large skillet or sauté pan over high heat, add the ground beef, and cook, breaking it up with a spoon, until it is browned and cooked. Remove from the pan and set aside in a bowl. Wipe the pan dry.

Heat the remaining 3 tablespoons olive oil over medium-high heat in the same pan. Add the onion, celery, carrot, and pancetta, then season with salt and pepper. Cook, stirring occasionally, until the vegetables soften and then caramelize; you want them to intensify in sweetness and depth of flavor. Stir it occasionally. Don't scorch it; just take it to this side of brown.

Add the wine and stir until it cooks off. Stir in the tomatoes and the cooked beef and drop the heat to medium or whatever level it takes to keep it at a steady fry/simmer for the better part of half an hour. You gotta keep an eye on this, because you don't want it to burn or dry out. Add a few tablespoons water if it starts to dry out. If it starts to burn, drop the heat a bit. You want to maximize the caramel, not the carbon. Ideally, the sauce should be rich and a bit on the dry side in the end (this is not about soaking the noodles, it's about just coating them with a rich, meaty sauce that clings to the noodle). Serve with the cooked pasta of your choice.

bacon is better

While classic bolognese takes time, time, time, the addition of cured pork adds deepness of flavor that is unparalleled and un-time-consuming. Further proof that cured pork is the cure.

"Fresh
marjoran
is like an
amped-up
version
of oregano
and
definitely
worth
working
into
your
repertoire."

CHERRY TOMATO PASTA **WITH MARJORAM**

This pasta gets a bold flavor from marjoram, the fresh herb that's like an amped-up version of oregano. If you can't find marjoram, fresh oregano or another fresh herb will do, but this underappreciated herb is definitely worth seeking out and working into your repertoire.

Makes 4 Servings.

- 1 pound pasta (farfalle's curves and crevices grab the tomatoes nicely)
- Olive oil
- 2 garlic cloves, thinly sliced
- 3 cups cherry or grape tomatoes, or a mix of the two
- Fresh marjoram (or other herbs such as parsley, basil, whatever)
- Salt
- Freshly ground black pepper
- Parmesan cheese

Bring a large pot of salted water to a boil. Add the pasta and cook until al dente, following the directions on the box, and reserving about ½ cup of the pasta cooking water.

Meanwhile, heat some olive oil in a large skillet or sauté pan over medium heat. Add the garlic and cook, stirring, for a minute until fragrant. Add the tomatoes, fresh herbs, and salt and pepper and cook, stirring, until the tomatoes have burst and broken down a bit, about 8 minutes. Add enough drained pasta, with a little of the reserved pasta cooking water, to the pan so that there's a nice ratio of tomatoes to pasta. Toss over heat until well sauced. Serve with a ton of Parmesan grated over it.

5-MINUTE **TOMATO SAUCE**

- 1 16-ounce can peeled plum tomatoes
- Olive oil
- 2 garlic cloves
- Salt
- Freshly ground black pepper

Who needs the jarred stuff when you can do it yourself without the sugar? Treat this as a base recipe for any herbal improvisation. You can dress it up with some toasted fennel seed added at the start, chile flakes, or any herb that suits the season (sage, rosemary, thyme, or parsley). Or add capers, olives, and chile flakes to make puttanesca.
Makes 4 Servings.

In a big bowl, carefully squish up the tomatoes. Add some olive oil to a medium saucepan over medium heat. Add the garlic and cook, stirring, for a minute until fragrant. Add the tomatoes and their juices and some salt and pepper and simmer, stirring occasionally, until it's reduced to a nice consistency, 10 to 12 minutes. Serve with the cooked pasta of your choice.

SPANISH **RICE**

A classic worth keeping in the repertoire. It's amazing what some olive oil and onion do for potentially dull white rice. Makes 4 Servings.

- Olive oil
- 1 medium onion, finely chopped
- 1½ cups long-grain or, even better, paella rice
- Salt
- Freshly ground black pepper
- Pinch of fresh cilantro

Bring a pot of 3 cups of water to a boil.

Meanwhile, heat some olive oil in a saucepan with a lid, then add the onion and stir to coat with the oil for 30 seconds. Next, add the rice and stir to coat with the oil. Cook, stirring, for 2 to 3 minutes, or until the onion has softened.

Add the boiling water and some salt and pepper to the rice and cover. Turn the heat to medium-low so that the rice simmers but doesn't boil over. In about 15 minutes it should be done. Garnish with cilantro.

spanish rice—the art of the sauté

What makes Spanish rice so soft and fluffy? The secret lies in sautéing the rice in olive oil and an onion for several minutes before adding any water. The high-heat oil coats and cooks each grain of rice, so that when you add water, each grain retains its character and doesn't stick to others.

QUICK PARSLEY & **PINE NUT PASTA SAUCE**

- 1 12-ounce package frozen cheese ravioli
- 4 tablespoons olive oil
- 2 cloves garlic, chopped
- ¼ cup pine nuts, toasted in a pan until light brown
- ¼ cup chopped fresh parsley
- Salt
- Freshly ground black pepper
- Freshly grated Parmesan cheese

Here's a quick sauce that came, as many of our recipes do, from necessity and an understocked pantry. We had frozen ravioli (though this works with any pasta you've got around). We had pine nuts in the cabinet. We had parsley in the fridge. We had little time. Hence . . . .

Makes 4 Servings.

In a large pot of boiling water, cook the ravioli according to the directions on the package and drain. Meanwhile, in a medium skillet, heat the olive oil over medium heat. Add the garlic and cook, stirring, until fragrant, about 3 minutes. Add the pine nuts, parsley, drained ravioli, and salt and pepper and heat through for about 5 minutes. Serve with freshly grated Parmesan.

"Improvisation is the soul of gastrokid. We had frozen ravioli. We had pine nuts. We had parsley. We had time..."

brown
Sauce

RAVIOLI WITH BROWN BUTTER, SAGE, & PARMESAN—A COLLABORATIVE **RECIPE FOR GASTROKIDS AND THEIR PARENTS**

- 1 10- to 12-ounce package cheese ravioli (frozen or fresh)
- ½ stick butter
- Bunch of sage
- Red pepper flakes (optional)
- Freshly grated Parmesan cheese

Okay. Butter. I know. But if you're not feeding your kid junk food every other day of the week, a little butter-sage sauce every two weeks is perfectly fine.

This recipe is a fun way of getting the kids to help out with the prep, as it needn't involve knives or much heat beyond the boiling water (which will remain your domain). Makes 4 Servings.

Bring a large pot of water to a boil on the back burner with the handle turned in, to keep kids from grabbing.

Let one of your kids open the package of ravioli, break them up into individual squares if needed, and put them on a plate. Let the kids cut up the butter with a dull knife as small as they can. Let the kids tear the sage.

Now you take over. First make sure to keep the kids away from the hot pan. In a medium skillet or sauté pan, melt the butter over medium heat and let it foam. When the foam subsides and the butter starts turning a pale brown, throw in the sage leaves and let them simmer a bit. Cook until the butter is nutty brown, then remove from the heat. If your kids can stand spice, throw in a pinch of red pepper flakes.

Grate up some Parmesan. Drain your ravioli, plate it, and spoon over the butter-sage sauce with those lovingly torn, rustic little pieces of herb. Then toss that Parm all over it and serve. Health food? No. Perfection? Yes. A Gastrofamily moment? Indeed.

! brown butter makes it better

While we advocate an "everything in moderation" approach to eating and feeding your family (beef once in a while, vegetables all the time, a cocktail without fail on friday, etc), we're happy to report that "everything" includes butter, and joyous that it also includes brown butter. We make brown butter once a month and add it to not only ravioli and other pastas, but sometimes drizzle it on vegetables and fish with a squeeze of lemon juice for balance. You can pretty much put it on anything sweet or savory for a caramely richness. A sprinkle of salt always helps. Just heat 4 or so tablespoons of butter over medium heat in a pan until it foams, subsides, and turns a nutty color—this can take around 5 minutes or so. Keep an eye on it and make sure it turns just a nutty brown. If you see black specks in it, it's gone too far. No worries. Just toss it out and try again . . .

pizza
Parcheezy's
delivers

PIZZA

Of the few dishes universally beloved by children, pizza is perhaps the most powerful of all. Exploit the inborn penchant for pizza, and take your kids' palates where they've never been before by substituting more adventurous toppings here and there: garlicky eggplant instead of sausage; pancetta for pepperoni; sage for basil. In our households, we eat on average one pizza per week: we try various cheeses, experiment with topping-to-sauce ratios, use up leftover vegetables (or that stray piece of bacon), and are always surprised and pleased with the outcome.

Pizza can help your kids' palates evolve. We've successfully introduced anchovies through pizza, and even broccolini (closely allied with pancetta on the pie, admittedly). Something about the comfort zone of a pizza crust gives your kids' taste buds license to explore.

BASIC PIZZA **DOUGH**

All of the ideas that follow start with the same base: a premade or homemade pizza dough stretched out onto an oiled cookie sheet; an oven preheated to 425°F; and a hungry family in a good mood because they know they're having homemade pizza for dinner. The main thing is to really stretch it out on the sheet so that it nearly meets the edges. Too thick and the dough will be too bready. Don't worry about making it circular: we actually think that a rustic rectangle has a more authentic air to it. Makes enough dough for 1 pizza.

- ¾ cup warm water
- 1 tablespoon milk
- 2 teaspoons active dry yeast
- 2 cups all-purpose flour
- ½ teaspoons salt
- 3 tablespoons olive oil

In a large bowl, combine the water, milk, and yeast and stir. Add the flour, salt, and olive oil and mix it all up until it begins to form a messy sort of ball of dough.

Flour the counter or table, place the dough on the surface, and start kneading. Fold the dough on itself and knead that. Fold again and knead that. Keep going until it becomes smooth. This might take 5 to 10 minutes, depending on your strength and stamina!

Rub the inside surface of a large metal bowl with a little olive oil, and place the dough ball inside. Cover the bowl with a kitchen towel, put it in a warm place, and let the dough rise. In about 1½ hours or so, it will get pretty darned big.

Here's the fun part: punch down the middle with your fist (or let your kid do this!). Turn the dough over so it's a smooth ball, cover again with a kitchen towel, and let it rise another hour. Now you're ready to cook pizza.

"Any hungry, cranky family will be instantly put in a good mood by the promise of homemade pizza for dinner. Buy premade, or make your own, and **you've got it, ahem, made.**"

THE PLEASE-THE-ENTIRE-FAMILY **THREE-ZONE PIZZA**

We've gotten into the habit of making multiple-zone pizzas like this one. Think of it as a sort of tasting menu of pizzas, or "trio of pizzas" to use restaurant parlance. In reality it can either satisfy everyone or introduce picky eaters to new flavors, as it did in this case. Makes 4 Servings.

1 recipe Basic Pizza Dough (page 122, or ever happy to cheat, we use Trader Joe's premade pizza dough—the white, not the wheat, which has a more intense flavor that's not compatible with as many toppings)
Olive oil
2 cups shredded mozzarella or 4-cheese blend

FOR ZONE 1
5 oil-packed anchovies (preferably the jarred kind from Spain or Italy), chopped into ¼-inch pieces
3 cloves thinly sliced garlic
¼ cup thinly sliced white onion
Generous pinch red pepper flakes

FOR ZONE 2
¼ cup thinly sliced white onion (sweeter types like Maui onions usually don't get much of a complaint)
5 fresh sage leaves, torn into ½-inch pieces
Many generous grindings of fresh black pepper (okay, preferably Tellicherry, but that's going a bit too far)

FOR ZONE 3
(Just the cheese)

Preheat the oven to 425°F. Stretch the dough out into a rustic, free-form rectangular shape on an olive-oiled baking sheet. This might take a bit of manipulation and time, but it's important to make it as thin and wide as possible. Spread the cheese thinly all over. Top each of the 3 zones with the ingredients listed.

Bake for 20 minutes or so, until it's as gorgeous as you'd like it to be. You know, brown and crispy on the edges, and everything else bubbling and happy.

! easy side dish

On a separate baking sheet on the lower rack of the oven, add a bit of olive oil, a mess of broccolini, chopped garlic, salt, and pepper, toss, and then roast at the same time as you bake the pizza. Stir with tongs midway through. We like them charred a bit. This might take 10 to 15 minutes.

SAVORY **PIZZA**

- 1 recipe Basic Pizza Dough (page 122, or store-bought premade pizza dough)
- Olive oil
- 2 cups shredded mozzarella or 4-cheese blend, or whatever cheese you and the kids like
- 3 tablespoons fresh savory (or oregano, marjoram, or whatever fresh herb you want to introduce your children to), plucked off the stem
- 1 cup halved cherry tomatoes

This pizza is savory. Literally. If made it with a ton of the herb called savory (kind of like marjoram, sort of like oregano, a bit like tarragon), along with some cherry tomatoes and cheese. Not much else. Just a 425°F oven, some premade Trader Joe's Pizza dough, and olive oil on the pan. Makes 4 Servings.

Preheat the oven to 425°F. Stretch the dough out into a rustic, free-form shape on an olive-oiled baking sheet. This might take a bit of manipulation and time, but it's important to make it as thin and wide as possible. Spread the cheese thinly all over. Top with the herbs and tomatoes.

Bake the pizza until golden and bubbly, about 25 minutes. Serve, but watch out: those tomatoes are lethally hot at first.

TWO-ZONE SHIITAKE MUSHROOM **& PLUM TOMATO PIZZA**

Here's a two-zone pizza inspired by two ingredients that always seem to be in the grocery store, no matter what the season. It's not die-hard locavore, but sometimes all you want is a mushroom-and-tomato pizza, no matter what the season. Makes 4 Servings.

- 1 recipe Basic Pizza Dough (page 122, or ever happy to cheat, we use Trader Joe's premade pizza dough, the white, not the wheat)
- Olive oil
- 1½ cups shredded mozzarella or 4-cheese blend
- Salt
- Freshly ground black pepper

FOR ZONE 1

Several plum tomatoes, thinly sliced

Several meaty shiitake mushrooms, thinly sliced

FOR ZONE 2

(just the cheese)

Preheat the oven to 425°F. Stretch the dough out into a rustic, free-form rectangular shape on an olive-oiled baking sheet. This might take a bit of manipulation and time, but it's important to make it as thin and wide as possible. Spread the cheese thinly all over. Top Zone 1 with the tomatoes and mushrooms. Season all over with salt and pepper.

Bake for 20 minutes or so, until it's as gorgeous as you'd like it to be. You know, brown and crispy on the edges, and everything else bubbling and happy.

just add water

Sometimes your pizza desire gets ahead of your vegetable drawer. To avoid topless pizza, keep a supply of dried mushrooms on hand. They keep forever and are there when you need them. Soak for 20 minutes in hot water, squeeze out the excess moisture, and you're tops.

GREEN ZEBRA **PIZZA**

Green zebra tomatoes do have just about the coolest name of any food. They're pretty tart, thus are a nice balance to the cheese. They're not too watery either, so they won't make your pizza soggy. Makes 4 Servings.

- 1 recipe Basic Pizza Dough (page 122, or store-bought premade pizza dough)
- Olive oil
- 2 cups shredded mozzarella or 4-cheese blend, or whatever cheese you and the kids like
- Fresh thyme leaves
- A few thinly sliced green zebra tomatoes

Preheat the oven to 425°F. Stretch the dough out into a rustic, free-form shape on an olive-oiled baking sheet. This might take a bit of manipulation and time, but it's important to make it as thin and wide as possible. Spread the cheese thinly all over. Top with the thyme and tomatoes.

Bake the pizza until golden and bubbly, about 25 minutes.

!

anatomy of an heirloom

Black Brandywine, German Giant, Big Rainbow, Box Car Willie, and Cherokee Purple . . . these are the names that evoke the horticultural history of heirloom tomatoes. These tomatoes are always organic and can trace their heritage back at least 50 years to a single variety. But now the irony: our favorite named variety—the green zebra—isn't an heirloom at all but rather a young upstart hybrid version of four stately tomatoes. While it's well named and pretty, it tends toward a low-sugar tartness that kids don't necessarily adore, though it's a great counterpoint to rich cheese.

ANCHOVY, CAPER, **& TOMATO PIZZA**

No cheese necessary for this briny beautiful pizza that is evocative of the side streets of Marseille. Makes 4 Servings.

- 1 recipe Basic Pizza Dough (page 122, or store-bought premade pizza dough)
- Olive oil
- 6 or so anchovies, drained and chopped
- 3 tablespoons or so capers, drained
- 1 cup or so canned peeled plum tomatoes, chopped and drained of excess juice (save the rest of the can for pasta sauce)

Preheat the oven to 425°F. Stretch the dough out into a rustic, free-form shape on an olive-oiled baking sheet. This might take a bit of manipulation and time, but it's important to make it as thin and wide as possible. Top with the anchovies, capers, and tomatoes.

Bake the pizza until the edges are nice and browned, about 25 minutes.

GRILLED LEEK & OLIVE PIZZA

This one is an argument for grilling too many vegetables one night, and then making a pizza the next day: we thinly sliced the leeks and cut the olives in half (we used jarred kalamatas). You could just as easily use the toppings on pasta, tossed with grated Parmesan and olive oil.
Makes 4 Servings.

- 1 recipe Basic Pizza Dough (page 122, or store-bought premade pizza dough)
- Olive oil
- 1 cup shredded mozzarella or 4-cheese blend, or whatever cheese you and the kids like
- A couple cups sliced, grilled leeks
- ¼ cup chopped kalamata olives

Preheat the oven to 425°F. Stretch the dough out into a rustic, free-form shape on an olive-oiled baking sheet. This might take a bit of manipulation and time, but it's important to make it as thin and wide as possible. Top with the cheese, leeks, and olives.

Bake the pizza until golden and bubbly, about 25 minutes.

all about olives

Who has the best olives? It's the sort of discussion that can raise the temperature of even the hottest Mediterranean clime. We're not about to enter that fray, but what we can do is offer a mini-guide to the olive family.

Arbequinas: Spain—small, slightly bitter bite
Beldi: Morocco—brine-cured and often used in cooking
Bitetto: Italy—sweet with an almond taste
Cerignola: Italy—meaty, mild, and bright green
Gaeta: Italy—salty, small, and brownish-purple
Kalamata: Greece—purple-black in color and smoky, rich in flavor
Manzanilla: Spain—medium-sized, green, and crisp; often stuffed with red peppers or brined anchovies
Sevillano: Spain—large, green, mild, and crisp
Niçoise: France—tiny, meaty olives tree-ripened to create their intensely rich flavor
Picholine: France—green olives with sharp, tart flavor

BACON & ONION **TARTE FLAMBÉ**

This is one of those basic flavor combinations that will set you up for life: thinly sliced onions that caramelize in the high heat of an oven primed for pizza; smoky bacon; and creamy crème fraîche that melts into the dough. It isn't health food by any means, but it is proof positive that pizza needn't involve tomatoes. The fresh thyme, if you have it, has an herbaceousness that contrasts nicely with the other flavors, but is by no means necessary; bacon can certainly pick up the slack. This is inspired by the flavors of the classic Alsatian tarte flambé.

Makes 4 Servings.

- 1 recipe Basic Pizza Dough (page 122, or store-bought premade pizza dough)
- Olive oil
- Crème fraîche
- 1 thinly sliced onion (white preferred, but red works too)
- Several slices bacon, chopped in ½-inch pieces or whatever size you like
- Fresh thyme

Preheat the oven to 425°F. Stretch the dough out into a rustic, free-form shape on an olive-oiled baking sheet. This might take a bit of manipulation and time, but it's important to make it as thin and wide as possible. Spread the crème fraîche on the dough. Top with the onion, bacon, and thyme.

Bake the pizza until the bacon is cooked, the onion slices brown a bit on the edges, and the crust is golden, about 25 minutes.

"While we
love pork
loin and
chops,
**nothing
beats
cured
pork**
(prosciutto,
speck,
pancetta,
or, yep,
bacon)
for that
little-goes-
a-long-way
pig power."

PANCETTA & **SAGE PIZZA**

- 1 recipe Basic Pizza Dough (page 122, or store-bought premade pizza dough)
- Olive oil
- A couple cups grated mozzarella
- 1 cup or so roughly chopped pancetta (or prosciutto)
- ¼ cup chopped fresh sage
- Freshly ground black pepper

Unsmoked pancetta is briny, porky purity. Sage is autumn personified (or herbified). Together they create an aromatic perfection in the house as they roast in the oven. Makes 4 Servings.

Preheat the oven to 425°F. Stretch the dough out into a rustic, free-form shape on an olive-oiled baking sheet. This might take a bit of manipulation and time, but it's important to make it as thin and wide as possible. Spread the cheese on the dough. Top with the pancetta, sage, and pepper.

Bake the pizza until golden and bubbly, about 25 minutes.

!

big on pig

We love pork for its flavorful fat, the sweetest, richest fat that ennobles all dishes it touches, from pizzas to sauces to sandwiches. While we love a loin or a chop, nothing beats a cured prosciutto, speck, or pancetta for that little-goes-a-long-way pig power.

ROSEMARY & BLACK OLIVE PIZZA

Hearty herb. Hearty vegetable. A perfect paring of strong flavors.
Makes 4 Servings.

- 1 recipe Basic Pizza Dough (page 122, or store-bought premade pizza dough)
- Olive oil
- 1 cup grated mozzarella
- ½ cup chopped black olives
- ¼ cup chopped fresh rosemary

Preheat the oven to 425°F. Stretch the dough out into a rustic, free-form shape on an olive-oiled baking sheet. This might take a bit of manipulation and time, but it's important to make it as thin and wide as possible. Top with the cheese, olives, and rosemary.

Bake the pizza until golden and bubbly, about 25 minutes.

FRESH MOZZARELLA, BASIL, **& TOMATO PIZZA**

- 1 recipe Basic Pizza Dough (page 122, or store-bought premade pizza dough)
- Olive oil
- 1 ball fresh mozzarella, thinly sliced
- Fresh basil, torn
- Fresh tomatoes, thinly sliced (plum are nice because they're not too watery)

The classic tricolor margherita pizza. Makes 4 Servings.

Preheat the oven to 425°F. Stretch the dough out into a rustic, free-form shape on an olive-oiled baking sheet. This might take a bit of manipulation and time, but it's important to make it as thin and wide as possible. Arrange the cheese slices on the dough. Top with the basil and tomatoes.

Bake the pizza until the mozzarella melts and the crust is brown, about 20 minutes.

!

thin is in

Want a doughy snack? Grab a doughnut. Want a pizza that maximizes flavor and texture contrast? Take the time to stretch the dough as thin as possible to let your seasonal ingredients shine. The thicker crust then becomes that much more of a treat.

breakfast

BREAKFAST

If the dinner table is a potential battleground, the breakfast table is guerilla warfare—no niceties, the pressures of school and work start times, undercaffeination, no baseline nourishment—which could lead a harried parent to cede defeat, which, though fully understandable, wouldn't be right. Instead, come up with a baseline repertoire of a few good tricks. One that we've developed in our household is the premade oatmeal batch. On a Monday morning, we make more than can be eaten. Instead of oatmeal for two, we make oatmeal for twelve and refrigerate the leftovers. Over the next few days, we spoon it up into individual bowls, microwave it, and serve it with milk, good dark maple syrup, and fresh fruit, and we've given our kids a seemingly freshly made, hot breakfast of whole grains. Add to that a poached or fried egg and/or a smoothie, and you've given your kid a head start that didn't involve boxed, overprocessed, oversugared cereals. Here are a few more tricks we've got up our sleeves.

HERBY THE **LOVE OMELET**

The lame B-movie reference will likely annoy and confound your children, but it does state what this omelet is all about: packing major flavor and nutrients into an omelet big enough for four to share. It's got the fresh herb thing, which must have a vitamin or two in it. It's got the classic tangy cheesy thing, which for some reason kids love. And it's got the egg thing, which is, well, cheap and easy. It's a classic midweek, oops-we-ran-out-of-ingredients dinner or weekend brunch (goat cheese and fresh herbs are things we keep on hand and replenish weekly; it's shocking how long flat-leaf parsley stays fresh in the crisper drawer). Serve with a chopped cherry tomato salad. **Makes 4 Servings.**

- Several stalks asparagus
- 6 large eggs
- Olive oil
- ½ cup crumbled goat cheese
- 2 cups chopped fresh parsley and basil leaves
- Salt
- Freshly ground black pepper

In a medium skillet over medium heat, add the asparagus and ½ cup water and simmer, covered, for 5 minutes or until the asparagus is tender. Drain the asparagus, chop into ½-inch pieces, and set aside.

Whisk up the eggs. Heat several tablespoons olive oil in a 10- or 12-inch nonstick skillet over medium heat. Pour in the eggs and cook for a couple of minutes, until the bottom sets. With a spatula, pull the far edge of the cooked egg mixture toward you while tilting the pan away from you, letting the uncooked egg mixture cover the pan. When this sets, do the same thing again. Then do it again. When the final layer is cooked through, place the goat cheese in a line down the center. Add the asparagus pieces, herbs, salt, and pepper. Using a spatula, and maybe a fork for assistance, roll it up. Let the cheese melt a bit. Slide onto a plate and cut into 4 pieces.

EGGS DE **LA VERA**

This is perhaps the most-requested egg dish in our household. The catchphrases are heat the pan; brown the butter; salt the eggs. This recipe employs the magical spice pimentón de la vera, the Spanish smoked paprika that every household should add to its spice cabinet. Makes 2 Servings.

2 or 3 tablespoons butter
¼ teaspoon pimentón de la vera (the dulce, or sweet, version; not picante, which is too hot!)
Salt
6 large eggs, beaten

Crank your flame to full-bore, high, searing, demonic heights. Put a large skillet over it and let it get really, really hot. Add the butter and watch it sizzle, foam, and eventually brown. Add the pimentón de la vera and salt. Then add the beaten eggs. Let them cook for several seconds. Once the edges have set a bit, use a spatula to pull the far edge of the eggs toward you across the pan, tilting the pan away from you; this lets the uncooked eggs on top flow forward onto the hot pan. Let those eggs set, then pull the far edge toward you again while tilting the pan. Do this repeatedly, until it's all cooked (it may only take 3 pull/tilts). If your pan is hot enough, this should take about 3 minutes total. Make sure it's all cooked through, then serve.

SMOOTHIE **OPERATOR**

Put on Sade's greatest hits. Imagine a world very, very distant from the one you inhabit now. Relax and face the fact that glamour and intrigue are for those who aren't worried about their kids coming down with scurvy or some other nutrient deficiency. Hence you're making a smoothie that will nourish on so many levels.

You needn't blow your family budget on hyper-seasonal fresh fruits that spoil uneaten due to the shifting sensitivities of juvenile palates (though you should of course introduce them to the pleasures of peak-season fruit when possible; just don't expect them to accept it with the fervor of a fruitarian). A smoothie usually goes down with a little more ease: it looks like a milk shake, tastes kind of like a milk shake (okay, not really), but it's actually fun to eat and can go back in the fridge for later if they bail on it at breakfast. You should drink one too.

Here's how to make it an easy, daily thing (need we say organic when possible?). Makes 4 Servings.

1. Each time you go to the grocery store, buy:
A few big containers of nonfat plain yogurt. It keeps for a long time.
A big orange juice
4 or 5 packages of frozen fruit (berries, mangoes, whatever)
A bunch of bananas

2. Buy a blender if you don't have one. (We burned out two $50 blenders in one year until we realized the $20 model does just as good a job. It just doesn't look as cool.)

3. Every morning load up the blender like this:
A few cups of frozen fruit in the bottom
A cut-up banana
A few cups of yogurt
A pour of orange juice

Let it sit there for 20 minutes while you do other stuff (it'll melt and meld and not make such a racket if you don't try to blend it while the fruit is frozen rock solid), then blend it up. If it's too thick, add more orange juice.

Serve in sippy cups with wide straws (before you get them dressed for school, because spills aren't very fun). It's a tasty fiber, vitamin, and protein foundation for the day. Will they feel better? Will you feel better?

"A simple
sunny side
up egg
gets even
the easy
addition
of our
favorite
red
smokey
secret
ingredient,
spanish
smoked
paprika."

EGGS DE LA VERA FOR ONE, **SUNNY SIDE UP**

A Gastroparent must remain flexible, which is how this dish variation was suddenly born: one day, Violet asked for Eggs de la Vera, but not scrambled (see previous recipe). A simple enough request. To be all super-foodie about this, it's a great study in contrasts: rich yolk in its purity (perfect for dipping toast into), neutral white as foil to intense pimentón. **Makes 1 Serving.**

Butter
1 large egg
Pimentón de la vera (the dulce, or sweet, version; not picante, which is too hot!)
Salt

In a small skillet, heat a little butter until foaming over medium heat, then slip in the single egg. Let it set on the bottom for about 3 minutes. Add ¼ teaspoon water and cover so that the top steams a bit, about 2 minutes more. Sprinkle with the pimentón and salt and serve with the yolk just cooked through.

!

bonus recipe: tartine

Such a French twist on yesterday's baguette: toast it up and slather with butter and jam. It takes something otherwise nearly useless and turns it into a culinary wonder—a revelation for kids and adults alike. The trick is to use a ton of butter and the best strawberry jam you can buy.

FAST FRENCH **TOAST RECIPE**

This is an excellent way of saving yourself the hassle of making a breakfast from scratch. Freeze the French toast, and heat it up in the toaster or toaster oven during the week. Makes 4 Servings.

- 4 large eggs, beaten
- ¼ cup or more milk
- ¼ teaspoon cinnamon
- A few gratings nutmeg
- Butter
- 12 or so pieces of bread

Beat the eggs in a bowl and add the milk, cinnamon, and nutmeg and whisk. Heat the butter in a large skillet over medium heat until it has foamed and subsided.

Dip the bread slices in the egg mixture until they soak up a bit of the goodness on both sides, and then fry without crowding the pan until the bread is browned and cooked through, a few minutes per side. Cool. Freeze. Toast up as needed and top with good, old-fashioned, deeply flavored grade B maple syrup (we think it tastes richer), or with a sprinkling of sugar—powdered or otherwise.

! bonus breakfast: blueberry pancakes

At Gastrokid headquarters, one of our favorite tweaks is organic frozen blueberries. Just throw a handful into the batter.

"We're not above using premade pancake mix, as the [illegible] **whole wheat varieties** provide sustenance and convenience without artificial ingredients. Make a **double batch**, refrigerate, and reheat on hurried weekday mornings."

.... and
a few more....

A FEW MORE

We like to cook. And when we say cook, we mean with heat: in a pan or on a stove with some great fresh produce that we can chop and transform. That usually has us bypassing the cold cuts, jarred spreads, and loaves of breads. Hence this is a chapter of odds and ends that fall outside of what we think is the realm of our favored methods of cooking. But these were just too delicious not to include, so here we have a few sandwiches (as if you couldn't make up your own), a refreshing drink, and a dessert that is so easy and delicious, you'll probably cook it once and start adapting it to fit into whatever glorious season you find yourself in.

THE PEANUT BUTTER **& JELLY BURRITO (PBJB)**

There's just one alteration and it makes all the difference: a whole wheat tortilla. Not a white one, mind you. You need something with a bit more character. Whole wheat it is. Oh yeah, there's another alteration: you microwave it. Not sauté it, not roast it, not bake it, not grill it. That's right: microwave it. On a plate. In a, that's right, microwave.

We used to roll up seven of these and freeze them at the start of the week (in a big freezer bag), then microwave them in the morning for the kids for breakfast. Okay, if you don't have a microwave, cook it the artisanal way, but then it loses its homemade frozen food instant appeal. Makes 1 Serving.

1 whole wheat tortilla
Natural peanut butter (not processed stuff like Jif or Skippy, both of which are loaded with sugar and other additives)
Fruit preserves

On a whole wheat tortilla, about an inch from one edge, spread a line of PB and a line of J. Roll it up tightly like a flauta, a flute, a tube, whatever. Microwave it. That's it. Let it cool a bit so you don't scald your child's tongue, but once they have a nicely cooled PBJB, they will forever clamor for these most excellent treats: for breakfast, for lunch, after school. You can also slice them up; the cross section has nice little jelly-roll/spiral look to it.

LATE SUMMER, **FAMILY-STYLE "BLT"**

It's a famously perfect formula. Even the bad ones are good. Crisp, salty sweet bacon, next to luscious sweet-sour tomato, next to crunchy neutral iceberg, against tangy, sweet, rich mayo, sandwiched between two pieces of toasted, yet yielding, sweet white bread. It's study in texture and flavor contrasts. And if this one (loaded with the platonic ideal of tomatoes and tons of fresh herbs) is the first one your kids have, it could just be the gateway sandwich to a lifetime of vegetable love.

This version substitutes purer, porkier Italian pancetta for bacon. It uses two varieties of tomatoes that bracket the range of tomato flavor: the ultra sweet and deep maroon Brandywine heirloom tomato, and the tarter, firmer green zebra (thinly sliced, so as not to overwhelm the other ingredients). The flavorless iceberg gets a spicy-sweet herbaceous replacement in a mix of arugula and basil. The bread is a step up from classic white: get a baguette and toast it slightly. Some things don't need to be improved: use the best mayo on the market, namely Hellman's (or Best Foods, as it's called on the West Coast).

This makes a family-sized sandwich that can be sliced into four pieces and served on a platter in all its glory. Makes 4 Servings.

- 1 big baguette, lightly toasted (under the broiler; careful it doesn't burn, oh exhausted parent!), sliced horizontally into top and bottom pieces
- Mayonnaise
- 8 pieces or so pancetta, crisped in a pan
- 2 big Brandywine tomatoes, thinly sliced
- 1 green zebra tomato, thinly sliced
- 1 bunch arugula, washed, dried, stems removed (or, even better, from a bag!)
- Handful of basil

Spread the bottom slice of baguette with mayo, then layer with pancetta, tomato slices, arugula, and basil. Spread mayo on the top slice of baguette. Close up the sandwich, slice into 4 smaller sandwiches, and serve.

Squeeze
Play
WHOLESOME
SWEETENERS
ORGANIC RAW
BLUE AGAVE
A Low Glycemic Organic Sweetener
AMBER
NET WT. 11.75 oz (333 g)

QUICK CACTUS **LIMEADE**

One day when Hugh's acid-loving son, Desmond, asked for limeade, Hugh made it way too tart. He was about to whip up some simple syrup to sweeten it (only a fool tries to dissolve granulated sugar in ice-cold liquid) when he saw a bottle of agave nectar in the cupboard. A squeeze of the stuff and the limeade was perfectly balanced. And Desmond loved the idea that he was basically drinking cactus juice.

Makes 4 Servings.

- 4 cups water
- Juice of 10 Mexican or key limes (regular limes are fine too, but only use 6 since they're much juicier)
- 4 tablespoons agave nectar (or more or less to taste)

Stir it. Ice it. Drink it.

VIOLET'S **CRUMBLE**

Hugh's nearly fruitarian daughter, Violet, loves any seasonal fruit cooked this rustic and easy way—particularly stone fruit and berries. Peaches and raspberries. Peaches and blueberries. This could also work just as deliciously with apples (use walnuts instead of almonds in that case). Rhubarb'd be good too, but would need way more sugar. Serve warm with a scoop of vanilla ice cream to take it over the top.
Makes 4 Servings.

- ½ cup almonds
- 1 cup flour
- ¼ cup brown sugar
- ¼ cup sugar, plus a bit more to sprinkle over fruit
- ⅛ teaspoon cinnamon
- 1 stick salted butter
- 2 cups sliced nectarines, cut into eighths or so
- 2 cups sliced strawberries, cored and halved or quartered depending on size

Preheat the oven to 375°F.

Chop the almonds in a food processor or with a knife until they're in little ¼-inch bits or so. In a large bowl, mix together the flour, sugars, and cinnamon. Cut the butter into chunks and work into the dry mix until crumbly, then mix in the almonds.

In a baking dish, spread the nectarines and strawberries, sprinkle with sugar, and mix. Top with the crumble mixture. Bake for 30 to 45 minutes, until the fruit is tender and the topping is golden brown.

Violet's crumble

PERFECT **PANINI**

A sandwich can be a harried thing during the week: slapped together, thrown in a plastic bag, eaten wherever and whenever the schedule requires. But on the weekend it can become an entirely different thing, an almost languorous culinary project (okay, that's pushing it). Still, on the weekend, everything does slow down a bit and a sandwich can be truly cooked, constructed, assembled, and elevated. It can be a panini, that romantic Italian preparation we've all fallen for.

It's something kids can help with and it teaches them a bit about patience and process in the kitchen: waiting for that lovely transformation by heat, pressed in a machine or between two heavy pans on the stove, all gooey and melty and melded. There's virtually nothing more comforting during fall. Here are two favorites that the kids (and adults) adore.

$2 Panini
Press

THE BRIT **PANINI**

7-grain bread
A bit of hearty mustard (only the slightest hint; you want a little acid and heat balance, not a full-bore blast that could turn off timid palates)
Sharp cheddar, preferably English but any will do (the high-fat stuff melts up better than the low-fat)
Arugula (the Brits call it rocket; the kids might like that)

This is an homage to Matthew's upbringing in Wales, where sharp English cheddar melted on a buttery grilled cheese was the taste of childhood. Makes 1 Serving.

Heat a heavy skillet over medium-low heat. Spread two slices of bread with a bit of mustard. On one slice, layer cheese and arugula and then top with remaining slice of bread. Place the sandwich on the pan. Place another heavy pan on top to press it down. Cook for a few minutes, taking care to toast but not burn the sandwich. Wearing an oven mitt, remove the top pan. Flip the sandwich, replace the top pan, and cook until all melty and melded. (Obviously, you could also do this in a fancy panini press instead, if you own one.)

! fried prosciutto-wrapped caprese panini-ini

My kids rejected a usually favored sandwich one day: a mozzarella, basil, tomato, balsamic, baguette thing we buy from a local sandwich spot now and again. So for dinner I cooked up some tortellini, sauced it with pesto, and served that with halved cherry tomatoes. After they were in bed, and after I'd eaten most of the sandwich they'd rejected, I had this hankering for something a bit more forward in flavor, something more intense, something good to eat with the dregs of my bottle of cheap Barbera d'Alba. I remembered we had some prosciutto in the fridge. I cut off a 1-inch piece of the sandwich, wrapped it in the prosciutto, and sautéed it, browning it on all sides. The cheese melted a bit, everything wilted, the prosciutto crisped up. It was perhaps the most delicious four bites of food I'd eaten in the past month. If you love Monte Christo sandwiches, you will worship the glory of this fresh, unctuous, porky, salty, crunchy, starchy treat. Next time I have a party, I will wrap an entire foot-long caprese sandwich in prosciutto, fry the whole thing, slice it up, and serve it as an appetizer.

THE YUPPIE **PANINI**

While the ingredients are French-ish/European-ish in origin, this sandwich is about as 1980s American yuppie as you can get when it comes to the ingredients, which, hilariously, have become new favorites among kids. The tangy goat cheese perfectly contrasts the sweet intensity of the sun-dried tomatoes. Makes 1 Serving.

- Rustic country white bread
- Goat cheese
- Sun-dried tomatoes from a jar, drained of most of their oil, but with a bit left on for that richness you want
- Fresh basil (or flat-leaf Italian parsley pulled off the stem; I know, it's nothing like basil, but it's green and plays nicely against the sweetness of the ingredients)

Heat a heavy skillet over medium-low heat. On one slice of bread, spread goat cheese. Then top with sun-dried tomatoes and fresh basil. Top with more cheese. Place the sandwich on the pan. Place another heavy pan on top to press it down. Cook for a few minutes, taking care to toast but not burn the sandwich. Wearing an oven mitt, remove the top pan. Flip the sandwich, replace the top pan, and cook until all melty and melded. (Obviously, you could also do this in a fancy panini press, if you own one.)

INDEX